Innovating Education & Workshops With AI

Harnessing Generative AI for Impactful Learning

Dr. Debora Bartoo

Copyright © 2024 Debora Bartoo

Debora Bartoo

db_book@yahoo.com

Printed and bound in the United States of America

First Edition, First Printing

Table of Contents

Introduction

W elcome to the future of learning, where incorporating new tools and content development are taking center stage for effectively creating courses and workshop designs with generative artificial intelligence (AI).

In the rapidly evolving landscape of education, the advent of AI heralds a new era of potential and possibility. This book is a comprehensive guide for navigating this exciting frontier. It is a crucial resource for educators, instructional designers, curriculum developers, and anyone involved in creating educational content and workshop development.

What You Will Learn

Understanding Generative AI

Delve into the world of generative AI, understanding its core principles, history, and how it differs from traditional forms of AI.

Practical Applications in Education
Explore the application of generative AI in educational settings, from creating dynamic content to personalizing learning experiences.

Designing Engaging Learning Experiences

Learn how to design courses and workshops that leverage AI for enhanced engagement, interaction, and learning effectiveness.

Navigating Ethical and Legal Terrain

Gain insight into the ethical considerations and legal frameworks surrounding the use of AI in education.

Future-Proofing Education

Look ahead to the future possibilities that generative AI may bring to the educational sector and prepare for emerging trends and technologies.

How This Book Applies to You

Whether you are crafting comprehensive courses or conducting workshops, this book offers valuable insights and practical strategies:

- **For Course Creators**: Understand how to integrate AI to enhance course content, tailor learning paths, and utilize data for continuous improvement.

- **For Workshop Facilitators**: Learn to employ AI tools for creating interactive and immersive workshop experiences, fostering collaboration and engagement.

- **For Educational Leaders**: Gain a strategic view of how AI can transform teaching and learning processes within your institution.

Key Benefits to Reading This Book

Example Use Cases: Draw inspiration from derived examples of AI in various educational settings.

Guidance: See practical, easy-to-follow instructions on using popular AI tools and technologies.

Insights: Gain insights from clear and meaningful examples to help understand the rapidly evolving field of AI, presenting opportunities for success in course design and workshop development.

Resources: Review a curated list of valuable resources, tools, and platforms for further exploration and learning.

Adaptations for a Workshop

Focus on Practical Application

Workshops are typically shorter in duration and more hands-on, but similar concepts throughout the book usually apply. Workshops tend to have more real-world applications and include interactive exercises throughout the event, including continuous engagement strategies. Feedback and reflection are a part of most education experiences.

The principles of structure, depth, application, and delivery in the chapters within this book remain similar for both longer courses and workshop strategies. Adapt these principles to align with a course or workshop's requirements and goals.

The Future is Now

This is more than just a book; it is a journey into the heart of modern educational innovation with AI. You are embarking on a course to understand this topic, its educational applications, and practical knowledge to implement these technologies in your educational endeavors. Join us in reshaping the teaching world, whether in traditional course development or workshop design, one AI-enhanced experience at a time.

Chapter 1:
Introduction to Generative AI

Understanding Generative AI

G enerative AI refers to a subset of artificial intelligence technologies that can generate new content, from text and images to music and programming code. Unlike traditional AI, which analyzes and interprets data, generative AI can create unique, original outputs based on learned patterns and data.

A Brief History

Researchers trace the roots of generative AI back to the early days of AI research, with significant advancements occurring through the development of neural networks and deep learning. Key milestones include:

- 1980s-1990s: Early neural networks laid the foundation.
- 2006: The term "deep learning" was coined, marking a renewed interest in neural networks.
- 2014: The introduction of Generative Adversarial Networks (GANs) revolutionized the field.
- 2018-onwards: Large language models like OpenAI's GPT series began demonstrating unprecedented capabilities in text generation.

How Generative AI Differs

Generative AI differs from other AI technologies' ability to create rather than analyze. Traditional AI systems, such as those used for data analysis or pattern recognition, are often called 'discriminative' models. They sort, categorize, and make predictions based on input data. In contrast, generative models, like GPT (Generative Pre-trained Transformer) or DALL-E, are trained to produce outputs that can be entirely new creations.

Core Principles

Learning from Data: Generative AI models learn from vast datasets, identifying patterns, styles, or structures. For example, a model trained in classical music can generate new compositions in a similar style.

Training Methods: We often train these models using unsupervised learning methods, enabling them to generate outputs without explicit instructions.

Iteration and Refinement: Generative AI refines its outputs through iterative processes. In GANs, for instance, two neural networks – one generating content and the other evaluating it – work to improve the output quality iteratively.

Implications for Education

Generative AI has the potential to revolutionize educational content creation and personalized learning. It can:

Generate Customized Learning Materials: Create tailored texts, problems, or examples based on specific curricula or student needs.

Enhance Interactive Learning: Provide responsive, AI-generated feedback or dialogue in educational software.

Inspire Creativity and Exploration: Serve as a tool for students to explore complex concepts through AI-generated models or simulations.

In the realm of education, the integration of AI-generated models and simulations presents a revolutionary approach to exploring complex concepts. These advanced tools open doors to immersive learning experiences, allowing students to delve deeper into subjects that were once challenging to grasp through traditional methods. Here is an expanded view of how AI can serve as a pivotal tool for fostering creativity and exploration among students:

Interactive Learning Environments

Real-World Simulations

AI can create simulations that mimic real-world scenarios, enabling students to explore and understand complex systems in environmental science, engineering, economics, or many other fields.

For example, students studying climate change can interact with simulations that model ecological impacts under different scenarios, helping them grasp the intricacies of climate systems.

Visualizing Abstract Concepts

Complex and abstract concepts, particularly in subjects like mathematics or physics, can be visualized through AI-powered models, making them more accessible and easier to comprehend.

AI tools can generate 3D models or interactive graphs to visualize concepts like fractals in mathematics or quantum mechanics in physics.

Enhancing Creativity

Art and Design

In art and design education, AI can assist in creating patterns, designs, or even entire art pieces, helping students learn about aesthetics, symmetry, and design principles in a hands-on way.

Music and Multimedia

AI-generated music and multimedia tools can help students compose music or create digital art, encouraging experimentation and creative expression.

Facilitating Scientific Exploration

Laboratory Simulations

In science education, AI can simulate laboratory experiments, allowing students to conduct experiments virtually that might be too dangerous, expensive, or impractical to perform in a real lab.

Creating lab simulations, including complex chemical reactions, physics experiments, biological processes, or even historical reenactments and economic models, can reduce potential risks and enhance understanding across various disciplines.

Data Analysis and Interpretation

AI tools can analyze large data sets, proving particularly beneficial in research-based projects across various fields like astronomy, genetics, social sciences, banking, retail, and healthcare. These tools offer valuable insights and efficiency in handling complex and voluminous data.

Enhancing Problem-Solving Skills

Scenario-Based Learning

AI can create scenario-based learning environments where students can solve real-world problems, enhancing their critical thinking and problem-solving skills.

For instance, in a business course, students could navigate an AI-generated market simulation to learn about economics and business strategies.

Interactive Storytelling

AI can create interactive and branching narratives, allowing students to explore different outcomes based on their decisions. This interactive storytelling method is advantageous in teaching subjects like history, literature, and ethics.

Conclusion – A New Dimension of Learning

As we delve deeper into the potential of generative AI in education, it is crucial to understand its foundational principles and historical context. Using AI-generated models and simulations in teaching or facilitating workshops is not just about technological advancement; it is about opening new dimensions of learning that are more interactive, engaging, and attuned to the complexities of the modern world. These tools make learning more dynamic and cater to various learning styles, encouraging students to explore, create, and think critically. Integrating these technologies into educational practices will pave the way for a generation of learners equipped to navigate and shape an increasingly complex world. This understanding will pave the way for effectively harnessing its capabilities in educational settings while also being mindful of its limitations and ethical considerations. We will explore these aspects in detail, guiding educators and educational leaders in integrating generative AI into their teaching and learning practices.

Chapter 2: Technologies Behind Generative AI

Simplifying the Complex: The Building Blocks of Generative AI

U nderstanding the core technologies behind generative AI can seem daunting, but at its heart, it is about teaching machines to create. This chapter breaks down these complex concepts into more digestible parts.

Neural Networks: The Foundation

What is a Neural Network?

Imagine a neural network as a complex web of decision points, mirroring how neurons in the human brain work. Each 'neuron' in this network processes a small piece of information, and together, they make a decision or prediction.

Layers of Learning

Neural networks consist of layers. The first layer receives the input (like an image or text), and the last gives the output. Between them are 'hidden layers' where most processing occurs.

Learning Through Examples

These networks learn through examples. When you show a neural network thousands of pictures of cats, it gradually learns the patterns that define what a cat looks like.

Deep Learning: Going Deeper into Data

Deep Learning Explained

'Deep' in deep learning refers to the number of layers in a neural network. More layers allow the network to understand complex patterns and subtleties in the data, which is essential for generating new content.

Why Deep Learning for Generative AI?

Deep learning is crucial for generative AI because it can handle and generate complex, high-dimensional data like images, sound, and text, which simpler models can't.

Generative Adversarial Networks (GANs): The Art of Mimicry

The GAN Framework

GANs consist of two neural networks: a generator and a discriminator. The generator creates content while the discriminator evaluates it. It's like a constant cat-and-mouse game, where each tries to outsmart the other.

Training GANs

During training, the generator learns to produce more realistic outputs, while the discriminator becomes better at telling genuine from fake. This adversarial process leads to high-quality generation.

Reinforcement Learning: Learning Through Trial and Error

Understanding Reinforcement Learning

Reinforcement learning is about taking action and learning from the outcomes. It is like teaching a child to ride a bike; they adjust their balance each time they tilt too far.

Reinforcement Learning: Applications in Adult Learning and Professional Development

Reinforcement learning, a key concept in AI, provides valuable insights and methodologies to apply in adult learning and professional development contexts effectively. Just as it operates in AI systems—where algorithms learn and improve based on feedback from their environment—reinforcement learning can be a powerful tool for adult education, enhancing skill acquisition and decision-making processes.

Applications of Reinforcement Learning in Workplace Training

Scenario-Based E-Learning

In professional settings, you can design e-learning modules using reinforcement learning principles, allowing learners to make decisions in simulated scenarios like managing a project or resolving a customer service issue.

The program provides immediate feedback based on their choices, reinforcing good practices and correcting mistakes.

Skill Acquisition and Mastery

You can apply reinforcement learning in training programs for skill development, such as sales training or technical skills. As adults practice these skills in real or simulated environments, they receive immediate feedback and results, reinforcing their learning.

Reinforcement Learning in Leadership Development

Decision-Making Simulations

For leadership development, you can use reinforcement learning in simulations that mimic complex decision-making scenarios leaders face, such as crisis management or strategic planning.

Leaders learn and refine their decision-making skills based on the outcomes of their actions in the simulation.

Feedback Loops in Coaching

Coaching sessions utilize reinforcement learning, where leaders receive regular feedback on their actions and decisions through methods like 360-degree feedback or performance metrics. These methods help leaders adjust and improve their leadership styles and strategies.

Continuous Professional Development

Personalized Learning Paths

In adult education, reinforcement learning can help in creating personalized learning paths. The system adapts to their learning pace and style as adult learners progress, providing targeted materials to reinforce their learning journey.

Microlearning and Gamification

Microlearning platforms can provide opportunities for reinforcement learning where adults receive bite-sized learning content combined with gamification elements. This approach reinforces learning in a manageable and engaging way.

Example: Medical Training Simulations

Medical professionals often use simulations for training in procedures and diagnostics. For instance, an AI-driven simulation for surgery training provides instant feedback on the accuracy of surgical techniques, allowing for real-time learning and improvement.

Application in Generative AI

In generative AI, reinforcement learning can fine-tune models, allowing the AI to receive feedback on its outputs and adjust for improvement.

Transformer Models: Revolutionizing Text Generation

What are Transformers?

Transformers are a type of neural network specially designed to handle sequential data, like sentences in a paragraph. They can understand the context and the relationships between words, making them excellent for language-based tasks.

Generative Pre-trained Transformers (GPT)

The transformer technology powers models like ChatGPT, which are trained on vast amounts of text data and can generate coherent, contextually relevant text.

Conclusion: The Symphony of Technologies

Generative AI is like a symphony where each technology plays a critical role. Neural networks provide the foundation, deep learning adds complexity, GANs bring creativity, reinforcement learning offers adaptability, and transformers introduce a deep understanding of language. Together, these technologies create generative AI's powerful and versatile tools, opening new horizons in educational possibilities. The following chapters will explore how these technologies can be applied in educational contexts, providing practical insights for educators and leaders.

Chapter 3:
Generative AI in Education

Unveiling the Role of Generative AI in the Learning Sphere

Generative AI is rapidly transforming the educational landscape. This chapter explores its multifaceted applications in education, offering educators a glimpse into a future where AI is a fundamental part of teaching and learning.

Personalized Learning: Tailoring Education to Each Learner

Customized Content Creation

Generative AI can create customized learning materials catering to students' needs and learning styles. For instance, it can generate text-based content that matches a student's reading level or interest.

Adaptive Learning Paths

AI can design personalized learning paths by assessing a student's performance and recommending tailored resources or exercises. This approach ensures that each student is challenged appropriately and receives support where needed.

Automated Content Generation: Enhancing Educational Materials

Generating Diverse Educational Resources

From crafting unique problem sets in math to generating case studies in social studies, generative AI can produce a vast array of educational materials, reducing the time educators spend on content creation.

Generative AI's potential to create a wide range of educational materials can be transformative, particularly in customizing learning experiences and enhancing the efficiency of content creation. Here is an example of how this can be accomplished, including the use of prompt technology:

Example: Customized Problem Sets in Mathematics

Defining the Scope with AI Prompts

Educators can start by defining the scope of the problem set using AI prompts. For instance, they might input: "Generate a set of 20 algebra problems for 10th-grade students, focusing on quadratic equations."

AI-Generated Problems

Using its database and algorithms, the AI generates diverse problems based on the input prompt. These problems can vary in difficulty and structure, ensuring a comprehensive understanding of the topic.

Incorporating Real-World Scenarios

Use further prompts to make problems more engaging, such as: "Include real-world applications and scenarios in at least five of the algebra problems."

Review and Refinement

The educator reviews the generated problems, making any necessary refinements or adjustments to align with their specific teaching goals or the needs of their students.

Case Studies in Social Studies

Utilizing AI for Case Study Development

An educator could use a prompt like: "Create a case study on the impact of industrialization on European societies in the 19th century."

The AI then drafts a comprehensive case study, pulling historical data, impacts, and relevant social theories.

Customization for Different Learning Levels

Adjust prompts to suit different educational levels. For example, for more advanced students, include prompts that involve specific economic theories or historical figures. This approach ensures the learning material remains challenging and relevant to the student's academic stage.

Integration of Interactive Elements

Use additional prompts to integrate multimedia elements or interactive questions within the case study, enhancing engagement. This method ensures a more dynamic and immersive learning experience for the students.

Advantages of Using Prompt Technology

Personalization: Prompt technology enables educators to specify precisely the type of content they need, tailored to the curriculum and student learning levels. This personalization ensures that the generated material aligns closely with the educational objectives and caters to the varied proficiency levels of students.

Efficiency: The tools can provide efficiencies and significantly reduce the time required to create diverse and comprehensive educational materials.

Variability and Creativity: AI can generate various examples and scenarios, often introducing creative approaches that might not occur in traditional content development. This capability enriches the learning material with diverse and innovative perspectives, enhancing the educational experience.

Language Translation and Localization

AI tools can automatically translate educational content into multiple languages, making knowledge more accessible globally and aiding in language learning.

Creating Interactive and Engaging Content

Generative AI can develop interactive simulations, games, and quizzes, making learning more engaging and effective.

Interactive Learning Tools: Engaging Students in New Ways

AI Tutors and Assistants

AI-driven tutors revolutionize independent learning by providing instant feedback, answering questions, and offering detailed explanations. These tutors are available around the clock, breaking the constraints of traditional classroom timings and allowing students to learn at their own pace. They use sophisticated algorithms to personalize the learning experience, adapting to each student's unique learning style and progress. This personalization ensures that students receive the most relevant guidance for their learning journey. Furthermore, AI tutors can track student progress over time, identifying areas of strength and those needing improvement, thus enabling a more targeted and efficient learning process. This innovative approach makes education more accessible and tailored to individual needs, transforming how knowledge is acquired and retained.

Enhancing Collaborative Learning

AI tools facilitate collaborative projects by suggesting ideas, providing research materials, moderating discussions, and fostering a collaborative learning environment. Their involvement enhances the efficiency and creativity of group work, making collaboration more dynamic and productive.

Creativity and Exploration: Expanding the Boundaries of Learning

Encouraging Creative Expression

Generative AI catalyzes creativity in art, music, and creative writing. Suggesting novel ideas and concepts can spark imagination and offer fresh perspectives. AI can generate diverse visual styles and compositions in art classes, providing students with a wide range of artistic inspirations. AI can create sample melodies or rhythms for music students, helping them explore different musical genres and techniques. AI can assist with plot development and character creation in creative writing or even provide examples of various writing styles. This technology can guide students through the creative process, offering suggestions that they can expand upon, refine, or even challenge. Generative AI helps students consider possibilities that have not been explored and push the boundaries of their creativity, leading to more innovative and diverse artistic expressions. This integration of AI in creative disciplines democratizes and enriches the creative process, making it more accessible and diverse.

Exploratory Learning and Problem-Solving

AI models simulate complex systems or problems, enabling students to explore and experiment in a virtual environment, a method especially valuable in science, technology, engineering, and mathematics (STEM) education. This approach enriches

STEM learning by providing practical, hands-on experiences in a controlled, virtual setting.

Assessment and Feedback: Streamlining Evaluation

Automated Grading Systems

AI can significantly streamline the grading process, particularly for objective assignments like quizzes. By automating the evaluation of multiple-choice questions, fill-in-the-blanks, and other standardized formats, AI systems can quickly and accurately assess student responses, providing immediate results. This automation frees up educators from the time-consuming task of grading these types of assignments, allowing them to devote more attention to subjective assessments like essays, projects, and oral presentations where personal judgment and feedback are crucial. Additionally, this shift enables educators to focus more on personalized teaching methods, such as one-on-one tutoring, mentoring, and developing customized learning materials that cater to individual student needs. By leveraging AI for routine grading tasks, educators can enhance the quality of their interactions with students, providing more in-depth guidance and support tailored to each student's learning journey. This balanced approach optimizes the use of technology and human expertise in the educational process, ensuring that students receive both the efficiency of AI and the irreplaceable personal touch of their teachers.

Personalized Feedback

Generative AI can provide personalized feedback on students' work, offering constructive reviews tailored to each student's learning journey.

Incorporating generative AI to provide personalized feedback represents a significant advancement in educational methodologies. This approach facilitates tailored, insightful feedback for each student, greatly enhancing the learning experience. Let us take a detailed look at how to accomplish this:

Implementation of Generative AI for Personalized Feedback

Integrating AI with Student Work Submissions

Integrating generative AI systems into digital platforms where students submit their work, like a Learning Management System (LMS) or an online portal, can significantly streamline and enrich the educational experience. This integration can be accomplished by embedding AI tools within these platforms to analyze student submissions for various factors such as content quality, originality, and adherence to assignment guidelines. For instance, AI can automatically evaluate and provide feedback on assignments, quizzes, and other coursework in an LMS, allowing immediate and personalized responses to student submissions. This speeds up the grading process and gives students timely insights into their performance, helping them promptly understand areas of improvement. Additionally, AI can facilitate more interactive learning by suggesting relevant resources, follow-up activities, or additional challenges based on the student's submission, creating a more dynamic and responsive learning environment. Such integration brings efficiency and engagement to the educational process, tailoring it to the needs and pace of each student, thereby making learning more effective and personalized.

Analysis of Student Submissions

Once a student submits an assignment, the AI analyzes the content based on pre-set criteria, such as clarity of argument, grasp of subject matter, or accuracy in problem-solving.

Advanced AI models can understand context and content, providing specific insights and suggestions.

Generating Feedback

The AI generates feedback personalized to the student's work, commenting on aspects such as the structure, use of sources, or argumentation in an essay. This process ensures tailored and relevant feedback for each student's submission.

In math or science, the AI could point out specific steps where a student might have gone wrong and provide hints or tips for improvement.

Incorporating Learning Histories

Generative AI can incorporate a student's past performances and learning trajectory into its feedback mechanism, ensuring that the feedback aligns with the specific assignment and the student's overall learning progress.

Personalization Aspects

Adaptive Feedback Based on Skill Level

The AI customizes feedback based on the student's demonstrated skill level. Beginners receive more basic, encouraging feedback, while advanced students get more detailed, critical insights.

Feedback Tone and Style Customization

Generative AI can adjust the tone and style of feedback to match the student's preferences or the educator's style, making it more approachable and effective.

Suggestions for Further Learning

Apart from assignment-specific feedback, the AI can suggest additional resources or activities to students, such as readings, practice problems, or tutorials tailored to their needs.

Challenges and Considerations

Accuracy and Reliability

Ensuring the accuracy and reliability of the AI system's feedback is crucial, necessitating regular calibration and monitoring. This process often involves periodic updates and adjustments to the AI algorithms based on student performance and feedback trends. By doing so, educators can maintain the system's effectiveness and ensure it continues to provide valuable, accurate feedback to students.

Human Oversight

While AI offers efficiency and personalization, human educators need to oversee its operation. They handle complex queries, provide emotional support, and ensure that the AI's feedback aligns appropriately with educational goals. This human involvement is crucial for maintaining the quality and relevance of AI-generated feedback and offering the nuanced support that AI alone cannot provide.

Conclusion: A New Era of Content Creation

Integrating generative AI and prompt technology in education significantly advances how educational content is created and delivered. It offers a level of personalization and efficiency that can substantially enhance both teaching and learning experiences. As these technologies continue to evolve, their integration into educational practices represents a forward-thinking approach, keeping pace with the changing landscape of education in the digital age.

Chapter 4:
Designing Courses with
Generative AI

Harnessing AI for Innovative Curriculum Development

This chapter provides educators and educational leaders practical guidance on integrating generative AI into course design. The aim is to create dynamic, engaging, and adaptive learning materials that cater to diverse student needs.

Understanding the Capabilities of Generative AI in Course Design

Adaptive Content Creation

Generative AI can create various content types, such as text, images, and interactive media, tailored to the course objectives and student profiles. Using multiple mediums helps to keep students engaged throughout the learning process.

Dynamic Curriculum Planning

AI tools can assist in designing curricula that adapt to the evolving needs of students and dynamics in an industry and incorporate real-time feedback and performance data.

Step-by-Step Guide to Integrating Generative AI

Setting Clear Objectives

Specify your goals for integrating AI into your course, such as enhancing student engagement or providing personalized learning experiences. Clearly defined objectives will guide the implementation process and help measure AI integration's success. These goals include improving assessment accuracy, increasing interactive learning opportunities, or tailoring content to individual student needs.

Selecting the Right AI Tools

Choose AI tools that align with your course objectives. Consider factors like ease of use, data privacy, and the type of content you want to generate, whether text, images, or multimedia.

Creating a Framework for AI Integration

Develop a structured plan outlining how you will use AI in your course, including determining which parts of the curriculum will receive AI assistance and how students and educators will utilize these tools. This plan should detail the integration of AI technologies into specific course segments and the expected roles of students and educators in engaging with these technologies.

Implementing Generative AI in Course Design

Developing AI-Generated Learning Materials

Use AI to create custom textbooks, lesson plans, and other educational resources tailored to various learning styles and levels. This approach allows for the development of materials specifically designed to meet the diverse needs of students.

Incorporating Interactive Elements

Enhance courses with AI-generated quizzes, simulations, and interactive discussions. These elements can make learning more engaging and effective.

Facilitating Personalized Learning Paths

Use AI to assess student performance and adapt the curriculum to individual learning needs, offering personalized resources and guidance.

Best Practices for Using Generative AI in Education

Ensuring Ethical Use of AI

Organizations are tasked with addressing ethical concerns such as data privacy and bias in AI-generated content, ensuring AI tools are used to respect student privacy and promote equity. Implement measures to safeguard personal data and regularly audit AI content for bias to maintain fairness and inclusivity in the learning environment.

Encouraging Human-AI Collaboration

Promote a balanced approach where AI complements traditional teaching methods rather than replacing human interaction and guidance.

Incorporating generative AI into educational settings offers vast potential, but it is most effective when used in collaboration with human educators, not as a replacement. This balanced approach leverages the strengths of both AI and human insight to enhance the learning experience. Let us take a detailed look at how to achieve human-AI collaboration:

Strategies for Human-AI Collaboration

AI as a Supportive Tool

Use AI to handle routine tasks like grading multiple-choice tests or monitoring student progress, allowing educators to focus on more complex teaching tasks and personalized student interactions.

Customized Content Creation

Educators can utilize AI to generate and tailor course materials but should refine and personalize them based on their expertise and understanding of the class's needs.

Augmenting Human Feedback

While AI can provide initial feedback on assignments, educators can add further insights, contextual understanding, and emotional intelligence to this feedback. The input from course or workshop facilitators brings value to students and aids in the learning process.

Interactive Learning Activities

AI can create dynamic learning activities or simulations, but educators should facilitate these activities, guiding discussions, encouraging critical thinking, and providing real-world context.

Blended Learning Environments

Blended learning environments can integrate AI-driven tools along with human teaching methods. Use AI to create adaptive learning paths and complement these with in-class discussions and hands-on activities led by educators. This approach combines the strengths of AI with the essential human element of teaching.

Balancing AI and Human Interaction

Enhancing Emotional and Social Learning

While AI can efficiently manage data-driven tasks, human educators are essential for teaching and nurturing emotional and social skills with participants.

Ethical Decision-Making and Creativity

Educators should guide students in ethical decision-making and creative thinking, areas where AI is limited. The goal is to ensure students do not entirely rely on AI but can use other educational means to continue to develop their skills.

Monitoring AI for Bias and Accuracy

Human oversight is necessary to monitor AI tools for potential biases and ensure the accuracy of the information and feedback they provide.

Professional Development for Educators

Professional development becomes vital for educators to understand and effectively use AI tools, enabling them to integrate these technologies into their work. This development might be driven by the organization where the individual works or their professional growth through many online or available courses or local meetups.

Collaborative Classroom Examples

AI-Generated Assessments with Human Insights

AI generates assessments based on the curriculum, but educators tailor these assessments to reflect the class's understanding and add questions that provoke higher-order thinking.

Tutoring and Mentorship

AI-driven tutoring systems can provide the opportunity to practice and reinforce concepts, while human educators provide mentorship, deeper insights, and support for complex problem-solving.

A Synergistic Approach

The key to successful human-AI collaboration in education lies in recognizing and harnessing the unique strengths of both. AI offers efficiency, personalization, and data-driven insights, while human educators bring context, empathy, and deep pedagogical knowledge. They can create a more nuanced, responsive, and effective educational experience. As we progress, the synergy between human and artificial intelligence will become a cornerstone of innovative educational practices.

Continuous Evaluation and Feedback

As with traditional courses and workshops, a regular assessment should incorporate the effectiveness of AI tools, and feedback should be sought from students and educators for continuous improvement.

Conclusion: The Future is Collaborative

Incorporating generative AI into course design offers a pathway to more personalized, dynamic, and engaging educational experiences. By understanding and leveraging the capabilities of these tools, educators can create innovative learning environments that educate and inspire students. The journey toward effective AI integration in education is ongoing, and as the field evolves, so will the strategies for its use in the classroom. The following chapters will explore examples of how generative AI can be used in action, providing further insights and inspiration for educators.

Chapter 5:
Ethical Considerations in AI in Education

Navigating the Ethical Landscape of AI in the Classroom

An area at the forefront of the industry is the ethical implications and challenges of integrating AI into educational settings. These are complex issues to be aware of as the technology moves forward. Awareness can help guide educators and leaders in navigating these complex issues responsibly.

Understanding the Ethical Dimensions of AI in Education

Data Privacy and Security

AI systems often require access to personal data. Understanding the implications of data collection, storage, and usage is vital to ensure compliance with laws like the General Data Protection Regulation (GDPR) and the Family Educational Rights and Privacy Act (FERPA). Consulting with appropriate legal and compliance authorities can provide knowledge and assistance.

Securing student data and maintaining confidentiality is crucial. As these technologies increasingly handle sensitive student information, including performance data, personal details, and learning preferences, robust security measures must be in place. Data confidentiality involves adhering to stringent data protection laws, employing encryption methods, and limiting access to authorized personnel only. Fostering a culture of security awareness aids in securing and protecting this information. By prioritizing data security and confidentiality, educational institutions and technology providers can build trust with students and parents, ensuring that the benefits of generative AI are realized safely and responsibly. This commitment to privacy protects individuals and upholds the integrity and credibility of educational programs leveraging AI technologies.

Bias and Fairness in AI Models

AI models, trained on historical data, can reflect, and amplify existing societal biases, impacting educational outcomes and perpetuating inequalities. For example, if an AI system is trained on data that lacks diversity, it may not accurately assess or support students from underrepresented backgrounds, leading to unfair educational experiences. This can manifest in biased content recommendations, unfair grading systems, or inadequate support for certain student groups.

To address this, strategies for identifying and mitigating bias in AI systems are crucial. One approach is to ensure diversity and inclusivity in training datasets. By incorporating a wide range of perspectives and experiences, the AI system can more accurately reflect and serve a diverse student body. Transparency in AI decision-making processes allows for greater scrutiny and accountability. Educators need to monitor AI for potential biases, ensuring they can critically assess AI recommendations and complement them with human judgment. By adopting these strategies, educational institutions can harness the benefits of AI while minimizing the risks of perpetuating existing inequalities.

The Impact on Traditional Teaching Methods

Balancing AI and Human Instruction

Balancing AI and traditional teaching methods is essential to ensure that education remains a holistic and human-centric experience. AI should function as a tool that enhances and streamlines the learning process, not one that diminishes the teacher's role or the value of direct human interaction. For instance, while AI can personalize learning at scale, human educators are crucial for understanding students' emotional and social development, contextualizing learning within a broader societal and ethical framework and fostering a classroom culture that encourages collaboration and empathy. Teachers' pedagogical expertise and emotional intelligence play a key role in interpreting and supplementing AI-generated insights, ensuring that education remains responsive to students' diverse and dynamic needs. Thus, a balanced approach where AI complements traditional teaching methods can lead to a more effective and enriching educational experience.

Ethical Deployment of AI in Education

Developing Ethical Guidelines

Create comprehensive guidelines for the ethical deployment of AI in education, aligning with core values of fairness, transparency, and inclusivity. Collaboratively develop these guidelines with diverse stakeholders, including educators, administrators, parents, and students. Focus on the diverse impacts of AI in education, such as data privacy, security, bias, and inequality. This collaborative approach ensures the guidelines are relevant to real-world educational needs and ethical considerations, fostering collective responsibility and trust. Keep the guidelines dynamic and evolving with AI advancements and changes in the educational landscape. Regularly review and update these guidelines to ensure they stay effective in promoting responsible AI use in educational settings. This adaptive and collaborative method is crucial for making AI a beneficial and equitable tool in education.

Inclusive Design and Accessibility

When developing AI tools for education, prioritize inclusive design and accessibility to cater to a diverse range of learners, including those with disabilities. Design these tools with universal accessibility, making them usable for students with different abilities and learning styles. Incorporate features like screen readers, voice commands, and adjustable interfaces to support visual, auditory, or motor impairments. Ensure AI algorithms are free from biases that could disadvantage any learner group, promoting equitable learning opportunities for all. By embedding accessibility and inclusivity from the start, AI tools can effectively meet different learners' varying needs and challenges, creating a supportive and empowering educational environment. This commitment to inclusive design improves learning experiences and upholds the broader goals of equity and fairness in education.

Promoting Digital Literacy

Incorporating AI into education brings a pressing need to concurrently teach digital literacy, preparing students to interact responsibly and effectively with advanced technologies. Digital literacy goes beyond basic computer skills, encompassing an understanding of how AI systems work, their capabilities, and their limitations. Educating students about the ethical use of AI, data privacy, and security is essential in this digital age. Students need to learn how to critically evaluate the information provided by AI systems and to understand the potential biases in AI algorithms. Digital literacy also involves teaching students about the impact of AI on society and future job markets, equipping them with the skills to adapt to a rapidly evolving digital world. By integrating digital literacy into the curriculum, educators ensure that students are not just passive consumers of technology but informed, critical, and responsible users. This holistic approach empowers students to navigate the digital landscape confidently and ethically, making them well-prepared for the challenges and opportunities of the future.

The Way Forward: Ethical AI in Education

Continuous Monitoring and Evaluation

Monitoring and evaluating AI tools in education is essential to ensure they meet ethical standards and educational goals. This process includes assessing AI's effectiveness, fairness, and impact on the learning environment. Gathering feedback from both educators and students is important to understand AI's practical implications and outcomes. Regular evaluations are crucial for identifying AI algorithm biases or issues facilitating continuous improvement. Such ongoing vigilance ensures that AI tools enhance learning experiences and maintain the highest ethical and educational integrity standards.

Collaboration and Dialogue

Open dialogue and collaboration among educators, technologists, policymakers, and other stakeholders are pivotal in navigating the ethical landscape of AI in education. Such collaboration fosters a multidisciplinary approach to addressing challenges, ensuring that decision-making processes consider diverse perspectives. Regular forums, roundtable discussions, and collaborative workshops can facilitate this exchange of ideas, allowing stakeholders to share insights and best practices. These interactions are crucial for developing comprehensive strategies that balance technological innovation with educational ethical considerations. Moreover, they contribute to creating a unified vision for AI's role in education, ensuring its deployment benefits all participants in the learning process. This collaborative ethos is vital to harnessing AI's potential responsibly and effectively.

Conclusion: A Responsible Approach to AI in Education

Integrating AI in education offers immense potential, but educators must navigate it with a strong ethical compass. Understanding and addressing the ethical implications ensures that AI's use in classrooms enriches learning experiences while upholding fairness, privacy, and inclusivity. The subsequent chapters will delve into practical examples and explore strategies for implementing AI in education in an ethically responsible manner.

Chapter 6:
Interactive Learning with
Chatbots and Virtual Assistants

Embracing AI-Driven Interactivity in Education

The adoption of AI-driven chatbots and virtual assistants has become the norm in many industries including education. Understanding these tools and how they can be incorporated into the learning experience can benefit students, including creating more interactive, engaging, and personalized learning experiences.

Chatbots and Virtual Assistants in Education

What Are Chatbots and Virtual Assistants?

Chatbots and virtual assistants are distinct yet closely related AI-driven tools designed to facilitate human-like interactions. Chatbots are specialized AI programs that simulate conversation with users, primarily through text-based interfaces. They are adept at handling specific queries and offering immediate, automated responses to standard questions.

Virtual assistants, on the other hand, are more advanced, incorporating voice recognition and natural language processing capabilities to perform various tasks. They engage in conversation and can execute tasks, provide personalized recommendations, and learn from user interactions to enhance their performance over time. While chatbots are often task-specific, virtual assistants offer a broader range of functionalities, acting more like personal digital assistants."

The Rise of Conversational AI in Education

Advancements in natural language processing (NLP) and machine learning drive the increasing adoption of conversational AI tools in educational contexts. NLP allows these tools to understand and interpret human language effectively, enabling more natural and meaningful interactions between students and AI. This technology transforms how educational content is delivered and personalized, making learning experiences more interactive and responsive to individual student needs.

Key Features of Educational Chatbots and Virtual Assistants

24/7 Availability

The round-the-clock accessibility of these AI tools allows students to learn and seek help outside traditional classroom hours.

Personalized Learning Assistance

Chatbots can tailor their interactions based on individual student needs and learning styles, providing customized explanations and resources.

Chatbots may be incorporated into a learning management system. A student struggling with algebra types in a question about quadratic equations: the chatbot, recognizing the student's learning history and past difficulties with algebra, provides a simplified explanation of the concept. It then suggests a series of step-by-step video tutorials and interactive quizzes tailored to the student's learning level. Additionally, the chatbot follows up over the next few days with more practice problems and periodically checks in to assess the student's understanding and progress.

Interactive and Engaging Learning

These tools can make learning more interactive and engaging through conversational and interactive elements.

Let us illustrate the use of interactive and engaging learning tools with examples:

Imagine a language learning app that uses an AI-driven chatbot. This chatbot engages users in interactive conversations, simulating real-life scenarios like ordering food in a restaurant or asking for directions in a foreign language. The chatbot responds to the user's input and incorporates games and challenges, adapting the difficulty level based on the user's responses. This approach makes learning a new language more engaging and practical, as users can practice conversational skills in a dynamic, interactive environment that mimics real-world interactions.

Examples of Chatbots and Virtual Assistants in Action

Generative AI in Education

Educators can utilize ChatGPT and similar systems like Google's Gemini (Bard) or IBM Watson, among others, in various educational scenarios. In tutoring, these AI solutions offer students personalized explanations and practice problems across a broad range of subjects. Acting as 24/7 virtual assistants, they answer academic queries instantly, clarify doubts, and guide research. For writing assistance, these tools help students with structure, grammar, and style, suggesting improvements and even generating essay outlines or drafts. The multifaceted application of these AI systems in education, including ChatGPT, enhances learning efficiency, provides accessible support, and aids in developing students' writing skills.

Virtual Teaching Assistants

Virtual assistants support teachers in administrative tasks, student assessment, and providing personalized feedback. For example, AI-powered assistants can manage class schedules, track student attendance, and organize educational resources. In student assessment, they help grade assignments and quizzes, saving teachers valuable time. Additionally, these assistants offer personalized feedback to students, tailoring responses based on individual performance and learning progress. This assistance streamlines administrative duties, enhances assessment accuracy, and personalizes student learning experiences.

Language Learning Bots

The following are insights on how chatbots aid language learning models, offering conversational practice and language exercises.

Table 6.1. Chatbot Applications

Category	Application	Example
ChatGPT in Education	Tutoring	High school students receive step-by-step guidance from ChatGPT in solving complex math problems.
	Answering Student Queries	ChatGPT, integrated into a university's learning portal, answers a wide range of student queries around the clock.
	Writing Assistance	ChatGPT assists in an English composition class by providing feedback on grammar, style, and structure.
Virtual Teaching Assistants	Administrative Tasks	Automates scheduling and resource management, allowing teachers more time for instructional duties.
	Student Assessment	Assists in grading objective assessments in a class, providing immediate results and analysis.
	Personalized Feedback	Generates personalized feedback reports for a history class, highlighting strengths and areas for improvement.

Category	Application	Example
Language Learning Bots	Conversational Practice	Engages users in Spanish conversational practice using realistic dialogues to enhance speaking skills.
	Language Exercises	Provides interactive grammar and vocabulary exercises, like fill-in-the-blanks, in a fun and engaging manner.

These AI models enhance educational contexts by demonstrating the potential benefits of AI integration in teaching and language acquisition. Explore how to tailor these tools to fit your specific educational needs, leveraging their capabilities to improve the overall learning experience.

Best Practices for Implementing Chatbots and Virtual Assistants

Seamless integration of chatbots and virtual assistants into the curriculum requires aligning these tools with learning objectives and outcomes. Educators should identify areas where AI can supplement traditional teaching methods, such as automating routine inquiries or providing additional support for complex topics. Integrating these tools is crucial to encourage interactive and student-centered learning rather than simply disseminating information. Planning collaborative activities using AI tools to develop facilitative techniques can enhance critical thinking and problem-solving skills. Moreover, regular assessment of the AI tool's impact on learning outcomes ensures its ongoing relevance and effectiveness in the curriculum.

Training Educators and Students

Effectively utilizing chatbots and virtual assistants in education requires comprehensive training for educators and students. Educators need to learn how to integrate these AI tools into their teaching methodologies and customize them for their classroom needs. Training should cover understanding the tool's capabilities, limitations, and the best ways to incorporate it into lesson plans. Orient students on how to interact effectively with these tools, helping them understand how they can supplement their learning process. Training should also cover digital literacy, ensuring users can responsibly and effectively engage with AI.

Ethical and Privacy Considerations

Addressing data privacy and ethical concerns is essential when implementing chatbots and virtual assistants. Ensure that AI tools comply with data protection laws and regulations, such as GDPR and FERPA, especially when handling sensitive student information. Educators and institutions should be transparent about how these AI tools use and secure student data. It is also important to regularly review and update privacy policies and practices in line with evolving technologies and regulations.

Additionally, it is crucial to foster an environment of ethical AI use in educational settings, where students learn the importance of data privacy and ethical interactions with technology, ensuring responsible AI deployment.

Challenges and Limitations

Recognizing Limitations

While AI-driven tools offer significant benefits in education, it is crucial to acknowledge their limitations, particularly in understanding context and nuance. Based on algorithms and data patterns, these tools may not fully grasp the subtleties of human communication or the complexity of certain educational concepts. This limitation underscores the continued need for human oversight and intervention. Educators play a vital role in interpreting and contextualizing AI-generated content, ensuring it aligns with pedagogical goals and student needs. Relying solely on AI can lead to gaps in understanding, making the educator's role in guiding, supplementing, and correcting AI content indispensable.

Managing Misinformation and Reliability

A major challenge in deploying AI tools in education is managing misinformation and ensuring the reliability of the information they provide. Given that AI systems learn from vast datasets, there is a risk of propagating inaccuracies or biases present in the training data. Educators and developers need to implement robust verification processes to validate the accuracy of AI-generated content, including cross-checking AI responses against credible sources and continually updating the AI's knowledge base. Educators should also teach students critical thinking skills to assess the reliability of information obtained from AI tools. Ensuring the credibility of AI in education is pivotal in maintaining trust and effectiveness in these technological advancements.

Conclusion: A New Frontier in Interactive Learning

Chatbots and virtual assistants represent a significant shift in how educational content can be delivered and experienced. By offering personalized, interactive, and accessible learning opportunities, these AI tools can potentially transform the educational landscape. As we continue to explore and refine their use, it is essential to balance their integration with a mindful approach to ethical considerations and the irreplaceable value of human interaction in education. The upcoming chapters will delve deeper into case studies and practical applications of these technologies in various educational settings.

Chapter 7:
Customizing AI Tools for Subjects

Tailoring AI to Enhance Subject-Specific Learning

T his chapter explores how educators can customize AI tools to enhance teaching and learning in various subjects as examples that can be applied to courses from mathematics and sciences to humanities and arts. The focus is on leveraging AI's versatility to meet the unique demands of each discipline.

Mathematics: Solving Problems with AI

In the rapidly evolving educational landscape, AI tools enhance problem-solving skills and deepen conceptual understanding, particularly in subjects like mathematics. AI can assist in solving mathematical problems and elucidate complex concepts, bolstering student understanding and proficiency.

AI-Powered Problem Solving

Step-by-Step Guidance

AI tools, particularly in mathematics, can break down problem-solving processes into understandable steps. For example, when a student inputs a calculus problem, the AI tool provides the solution and displays each calculation step, from differentiation to solving the equation.

Adaptive Problem Sets

These tools can generate problems tailored to a student's current skill level, adapting to complexity as the student progresses. This personalized approach ensures that students are neither under-challenged nor overwhelmed.

Instant Feedback

AI tools offer immediate feedback on problem-solving attempts. This instant response allows students to quickly understand their mistakes and learn the correct methodologies.

Enhancing Conceptual Understanding

Interactive Simulations

AI-driven simulations illustrate abstract mathematical concepts, such as geometric transformations or statistical distributions, making them tangible and easier to comprehend. These simulations provide a hands-on learning experience, enhancing students' understanding and retention of complex mathematical theories.

Visualization Tools

AI can create dynamic graphs, charts, and other visual aids to represent mathematical concepts, offering significant benefits for visual learners. These visual representations make abstract ideas more accessible and engaging, enhancing comprehension and retention. This approach caters to different learning styles, making mathematics more inclusive and understandable for a broader range of students.

Exploratory Learning Environments

AI creates exploratory learning environments where students can experiment with different variables and observe the outcomes, fostering deeper understanding through active engagement. This interactive approach allows students to learn by doing, making abstract concepts more concrete and understandable. Students develop critical thinking and problem-solving skills by manipulating variables and seeing real-time results. Additionally, such environments cater to various learning styles, making education more adaptable and personalized.

Real-World Applications

Connecting Concepts to Applications

AI tools are instrumental in bridging the gap between theoretical mathematical concepts and their real-world applications, enhancing students' understanding and appreciation of the subject. For instance, AI can simulate complex mathematical models used in economics, engineering, or environmental science, allowing students to see the practical impact of their theoretical knowledge. These tools can take abstract concepts like calculus or statistics and demonstrate their application in weather forecasting, architectural design, or financial modeling. Students gain a more practical understanding of mathematics by visualizing how equations and theories manifest in everyday scenarios.

A simple algebra example that can be created with generative AI demonstrating to the student how it is to be solved step-by-step:

Problem: Solve for x in the equation $2x+5=11$.

Solution:

1. Start with the equation: $2x+5=11$.

2. Subtract 5 from both sides to isolate the term with x: $2x+5-5=11-5$, which simplifies to $2x=6$.

3. Now, divide both sides by 2 which simplifies to $x=3$.

So, the solution is $x=3$.

Real-world application:

Scenario: Imagine you are shopping, and you have a coupon. This coupon gives you a discount of $5 on your total purchase. Let us say you want to buy several identical items, each priced at $2. You have a budget of $11. The question is: how many of these items can you buy within your budget, including the $5 discount from the coupon?

Application:

1. Each item costs $2, so if you buy x items, the total cost will be $2x$ dollars.

2. The coupon gives you a $5 discount.

3. Your total budget is $11.

So, the equation representing this situation is $2x+5=11$, where $2x$ is the total cost of the items, and 5 is the discount you are applying.

Solution: Following the steps we used before:

1. Start with $2x+5=11$.

2. Subtract 5 from both sides: $2x=11-5$, which simplifies to $2x=6$.

3. Divide both sides by 2: $x=2/6$, which simplifies to $x=3$.

So, you can buy 3 items with your $11 budget, taking into account the $5 discount from the coupon.

A benefit is that AI-driven interactive platforms can present students with real-world problems and guide them through applying mathematical concepts to solve them. This hands-on approach reinforces learning and encourages critical thinking and problem-solving skills. For example, students can use AI to analyze and interpret real data sets, draw conclusions, and make predictions based on their mathematical understanding. Such experiences make learning more engaging and relevant, showing students the tangible impact of mathematics on the world around them. By connecting classroom learning with real-life applications, AI helps demystify complex concepts and inspires a greater interest in the subject.

Problem-Solving in Context

AI-generated scenarios provide a unique and effective means of teaching students how to apply specific mathematical principles in contextually rich environments. By creating simulations of real-life situations, AI tools directly enable students to apply and test their mathematical knowledge in practical settings. For example, an AI system might generate a scenario where students must use geometry and algebra to design a functional bridge, integrating principles like load distribution and material strength.

These AI-driven scenarios can range from everyday problems, like budgeting and planning, to more complex challenges in fields such as astronomy or environmental science, where students might calculate trajectories or model climate change impacts. This contextual approach to problem-solving reinforces theoretical knowledge and develops students' ability to think critically and creatively.

Moreover, such scenarios can be tailored to the student's learning level, gradually increasing in complexity as their skills develop. This adaptive learning ensures that students are consistently challenged and engaged. AI-generated scenarios provide immediate feedback, enabling students to learn from mistakes and refine their problem-solving strategies in real time. This immersive and interactive approach transforms how AI tools teach and apply mathematical principles, making learning more dynamic and relevant to the real world.

Adaptive AI Systems in Personalized Education

AI systems demonstrate significant advancement in educational technology with their ability to adapt to individual students' proficiency levels, providing real-time personalized problem sets and feedback. This adaptability ensures that each student receives a customized learning experience, enhancing engagement and effectiveness. Adaptive AI systems are revolutionizing how education is personalized and delivered, focusing on their unique features and applications.

Tailoring Education to Individual Needs

Real-Time Proficiency Assessment

Adaptive AI systems continuously assess a student's proficiency in real-time, analyzing responses to determine their understanding and skill level.

This continuous assessment allows the AI to dynamically adjust the difficulty and focus of subsequent content, ensuring that it aligns with the student's current learning needs.

Personalized Learning Paths

These systems create individualized learning paths for each student based on ongoing proficiency assessments.

For instance, in a language course, the AI might focus more on vocabulary for one student while concentrating on grammatical structures for another, based on their respective needs.

Responsive Feedback Mechanisms

The feedback provided by these systems is not only immediate but also tailored to the specific errors or misconceptions exhibited by the student, involving explanations of concepts in different ways, offering additional examples, or suggesting targeted exercises.

Enhancing Engagement and Motivation

Gamified Learning Experiences

Many adaptive AI systems incorporate gamification elements, such as points, badges, and levels, tailored to the student's progress, enhancing engagement and motivation.

Interactive Challenges

Adaptive AI systems often present learning materials as interactive challenges, adjusting to the student's ability level to keep them both challenged and interested. For example, in a math course, the AI might offer increasingly complex problems as a student demonstrates mastery, ensuring the material remains engaging and appropriately challenging. This approach maintains student interest and promotes deeper understanding and retention by continuously pushing the boundaries of their knowledge and skills.

Supporting Diverse Learning Styles

Multimodal Content Delivery

Adaptive AI systems deliver content in multiple formats, including text, video, and interactive simulations, tailoring to what is most effective for each student's learning style. This multimodal approach ensures that students, whether visual, auditory, or kinesthetic learners, receive information in the best way they understand. By catering to different learning preferences, these AI systems enhance comprehension and engagement, making the educational experience more inclusive and effective for a diverse student population.

Incorporating Student Feedback

Students can actively provide feedback on the types of content and teaching methods that resonate best with them. The AI system can use this feedback to personalize the learning experience further. This continuous feedback loop and adaptation allows the AI to fine-tune its approach, catering more accurately to individual learning preferences and needs. Integrating student input makes AI more effective in delivering engaging and educationally valuable content.

Sciences: Exploring the World with AI

AI-Driven Simulations and Virtual Labs in Education

In the evolving education landscape, AI-driven simulations and virtual labs have emerged as vital tools, especially when physical resources or accessibility are limited. This section explores how these innovative technologies provide invaluable hands-on experience to students across various disciplines.

Bridging the Gap with Virtual Experiences

Realistic Lab Simulations

AI-powered virtual labs mimic real-life laboratory environments, allowing students to conduct experiments and procedures that would otherwise require expensive, specialized equipment. For instance, chemistry students can simulate chemical reactions, observing outcomes without physical risk or resource constraints.

Interactive Simulations in Complex Subjects

In subjects like physics or astronomy, AI-driven simulations can illustrate complex phenomena that are not readily observable in a physical classroom, such as gravitational forces or planetary motion.

Enhancing Practical Skills and Understanding

Skill Development in Safe Environments

Virtual labs provide a safe environment for practicing skills such as surgical techniques in medical training or circuit assembly in engineering, reducing the pressure and risk associated with real-life practice.

Immediate Feedback and Iterative Learning

These simulations offer immediate feedback, enabling students to learn from mistakes and iteratively improve their techniques.

Customizable and Scalable Learning

Tailoring to Curriculum Needs

Virtual labs and simulations provide highly customizable and scalable learning tools that align seamlessly with diverse curriculum goals across educational levels. Educators can tailor these platforms' content and complexity to fit specific teaching plans and student needs. For instance, they can adapt a virtual biology lab for different depths of study, ranging from basic cellular processes in high school to advanced molecular biology in college. This flexibility ensures that learning experiences meet diverse educational requirements and styles, efficiently accommodating large or multiple classes. Constant updates with the latest scientific advancements keep these tools relevant and forward-looking. By offering an interactive and adaptable learning approach, virtual labs and simulations enrich education and equip students with essential digital competencies for the future.

Scalability for Wider Access

The scalability of AI-driven virtual labs is a feature that democratizes education, providing equal learning opportunities to many students across different geographical locations. These virtual platforms can support large-scale access without physical lab resources, breaking down barriers related to location and infrastructure. This scalability ensures that students in remote or under-resourced areas have the same access to high-quality laboratory experiences as those in well-funded urban schools. Additionally, virtual labs can easily adjust to fluctuating class sizes or be deployed across multiple schools and institutions simultaneously, making them an efficient solution for broad educational outreach. By transcending physical and geographical limitations, AI-driven virtual labs play a crucial role in leveling the academic playing field, making advanced scientific learning accessible to all.

Data Analysis and Research

Integrating AI in data analysis and research has become a cornerstone in modern educational methodologies, particularly in enhancing students' ability to conduct complex research projects and experiments. AI algorithms excel at processing large volumes of scientific data, extracting meaningful patterns and insights that might be elusive to manual analysis. For instance, in environmental science, students can utilize AI to analyze climate change trends from decades of weather data, identifying significant climatic shifts and anomalies. In biology, AI helps understand genetic sequences and predict biological functions, aiding in cutting-edge research like drug discovery or disease analysis. These AI tools expedite the research process and enhance accuracy and depth of understanding. Furthermore, AI's predictive capabilities allow students to hypothesize and test scenarios in physics or economics, fostering a more profound and practical knowledge of theoretical concepts. Thus, AI in data analysis and research is not just a tool for simplification but a catalyst for innovation and discovery in student-led research.

Humanities: AI in Language, History, and Arts

Language Learning

AI tools are revolutionizing language learning by offering comprehensive practice options that range from grammar exercises to enhancing conversational skills. These tools use sophisticated algorithms to mimic natural language patterns, providing learners with an immersive and interactive experience. For example, AI-driven language apps enable users to practice pronunciation, vocabulary, and sentence structure through voice recognition technology, offering corrective feedback in real-time. This personalized approach helps learners memorize and apply language rules in practical, real-world contexts. Additionally, AI chatbots simulate conversational scenarios, allowing learners to practice speaking and listening skills in a safe, low-pressure environment. These AI tools are especially beneficial for learners who may not have access to native speakers, as they offer 24/7 access to a virtual language practice environment. The adaptability and interactivity of AI in language learning make it a powerful tool for breaking down language barriers and enhancing global communication skills.

Exploring History and Culture

AI's role in exploring history and culture is transformative, offering immersive experiences that bring historical events and cultural artifacts to life. Through AI-driven interactive storytelling and virtual tours, learners can virtually navigate ancient cities, explore archaeological sites, or walk through historical events, gaining a vivid understanding of different cultures and epochs. For instance, AI can recreate historical environments, allowing students to experience the atmosphere of ancient Rome or the bustle of a medieval marketplace. These virtual experiences become engaging stories by integrating narrative elements, providing context, and deepening the learner's connection with the past. Furthermore, AI-powered tools can analyze and present cultural artifacts in new ways, revealing hidden details or offering insights into their historical significance. This interactive and immersive approach to history and culture education enhances engagement and fosters a deeper appreciation and understanding of the world's rich heritage.

Arts and Creativity

The infusion of AI in art and creativity has opened new dimensions for artistic exploration, challenging conventional boundaries and inspiring innovation. AI algorithms can now generate unique art pieces and music compositions and even assist in creative writing by learning from existing styles and patterns while producing original works. AI can create stunning images and paintings in visual arts, blending techniques from various art movements to create something entirely novel. AI tools can compose pieces in different genres, providing musicians with inspiring base compositions to develop further. Moreover, AI aids writers by suggesting plot developments, character ideas, or writing styles based on the writer's input and preferences. These AI-driven creative processes serve as tools not only for artists but also as collaborators, offering fresh perspectives and possibilities. The result is a fusion of human creativity with machine intelligence, leading to unprecedented forms of artistic expression.

Interactive Case Studies

The application of AI in developing interactive case studies for subjects like economics, psychology, and sociology represents a significant advancement in educational methodology. AI can create dynamic models and scenarios that accurately simulate real-world situations, allowing students to delve into complex social, economic, and psychological phenomena. For example, in economics, AI-generated models can simulate market dynamics, enabling students to analyze the impacts of different economic policies or market conditions. AI can create scenarios in psychology that mimic human behavior or social interactions, providing practical insights into psychological theories. Similarly, in sociology, AI can model social systems and networks, allowing students to observe and study societal trends and behaviors. These interactive case studies are not just static representations; they respond and evolve based on student inputs, making learning a more engaging and immersive experience. By utilizing AI in this way, educators can offer students a deeper, more nuanced understanding of intricate concepts that are often challenging to grasp through traditional teaching methods alone.

Teacher Training and Professional Development

Effective integration of AI tools into educational practices necessitates focused teacher training and professional development. Such training programs should equip educators with the necessary knowledge and skills to utilize AI tools, ensuring they can enhance learning experiences without being overwhelmed by the technology. The curriculum of these programs must cover the technical aspects of using AI and pedagogical strategies for integrating AI in a way that complements traditional teaching methods. Additionally, continuous professional development opportunities are essential, as they help teachers stay abreast of the latest AI advancements and their applications in education. Ultimately, empowering educators through these training programs is crucial for AI's successful and meaningful adoption in the classroom, ensuring that technology facilitates innovative teaching and learning.

Conclusion: A New Paradigm in Education

Adaptive AI systems represent a paradigm shift in educational personalization. By providing real-time, personalized problem sets and feedback, these systems cater to each student's unique learning needs and styles, fostering a more effective and engaging learning environment. As these technologies continue to evolve, they promise to make education more responsive, inclusive, and effective for learners worldwide. Customizing AI tools for different subjects represents a significant advancement in educational technology. Educators can create more engaging, effective, and personalized student learning experiences by aligning AI capabilities with subject-specific needs. As AI technology evolves, its potential to transform education across various disciplines becomes increasingly evident. The following chapters will explore examples of ways to consider integrating AI course material.

Chapter 8:
Envisioning AI's Evolving Role

T he development of AI is moving rapidly, bringing with it the opportunity for a transformative impact on the educational landscape. Understanding how this can influence and impact new applications with emerging technology can aid in redefining teaching and learning.

Advanced Personalization and Adaptive Learning

Hyper-Personalized Learning Experiences

AI systems are at the forefront of creating hyper-personalized learning experiences, capable of adapting to each student's unique learning pace, style, and interests in real time. These intelligent systems analyze individual student interactions and performance data to tailor content, difficulty level, and learning pathways. For example, suppose a student struggles with a particular math concept. In that case, the system might receive additional practice problems in that area while it presents advanced challenges to another student who excels. AI also considers learning preferences, such as visual learning or interactive activities, to deliver content most effectively for each student. This level of personalization ensures that every learner receives an education tailored to their academic needs and aligned with their interests and learning styles, maximizing engagement and efficacy.

Predictive Analytics in Learning Pathways

Predictive analytics powered by AI plays a transformative role in education by foreseeing and addressing learning challenges and guiding students through personalized pathways. AI systems analyze historical and real-time data, identifying student learning behavior patterns, performance trends, and engagement levels. This analysis enables the AI to predict potential learning obstacles and intervene early with targeted support or resources. Additionally, AI can assess students' skills, strengths, and interests to recommend personalized career pathways, aligning educational goals with future career aspirations. For instance, a student showing aptitude in analytical skills may receive suggestions for data science or economics courses. This predictive approach not only enhances academic support but also aids students in making informed decisions about their educational and professional futures, aligning their learning journey with their evolving career goals. Immersive and Interactive Technologies

Virtual and Augmented Reality

Virtual Reality (VR) and Augmented Reality (AR) are two distinct yet complementary technologies revolutionizing educational experiences further enhanced by AI integration. VR immerses users in a wholly digital environment, a simulated world where they can interact with 3D spaces and objects. In contrast, AR overlays digital information onto the real world, augmenting physical environments with virtual elements. Combining AI with VR and AR brings a new level of immersion and interactivity to learning.

AI algorithms can enhance VR environments by simulating realistic and complex scenarios, such as a virtual laboratory for chemistry students to conduct experiments safely and interactively. Meanwhile, AI-augmented AR can bring historical events to life right before students' eyes, allowing them to witness history in their physical surroundings, enriched with interactive, digital information.

For instance, medical students could use AI-enhanced VR to practice surgical procedures in a realistic, risk-free virtual operating room. This experience is distinct from AR applications, where, for example, anatomy students might point their devices at a physical model to see layered information about human anatomy.

AI's role in personalizing these experiences provides significant benefits. In VR, AI can adjust the complexity of the virtual environment in real-time, while AR can provide context-specific information based on the user's interaction with the real world. This adaptive learning approach, whether in wholly virtual or augmented real-world settings, makes the learning experience more engaging and bridges the gap between theoretical knowledge and practical application.

Holographic Teachers and Classrooms

Integrating holographic technology with AI in education presents a vision of the future where classrooms transcend physical boundaries. Imagine holographic representations of teachers and experts projected into classrooms worldwide, providing students access to diverse global perspectives and expertise. This technology, powered by AI, could create realistic, three-dimensional projections of educators, allowing them to interact with students in real time, despite being physically located elsewhere. AI would enhance this experience by personalizing interactions and content delivery based on student responses and engagement levels. For instance, a renowned physicist could give a lecture from a university in one country to students in multiple locations worldwide, answering their questions and engaging in discussions as if they were physically present. This technology democratizes access to quality education and fosters a more connected and inclusive global learning community.

AI in Curriculum Development and Content Generation

Dynamic Curriculum Generation

AI systems dynamically generate and update curricular content in the ever-evolving educational landscape, ensuring its relevance and currency.

AI systems automatically integrate the latest scientific discoveries, global events, and cultural shifts into the curriculum, designed to keep the content up-to-date and relevant. For instance, an AI system could update a science curriculum to include recent breakthroughs in renewable energy technology or adjust a social studies curriculum following significant global events. This real-time updating ensures that educational content is not outdated, providing students with learning materials that reflect the latest developments and current affairs. Furthermore, AI can tailor this content to match the learning level and style of different classrooms, making education more adaptable and responsive to global dynamics and local needs. This approach to curriculum development keeps students informed and encourages them to engage with the world more informed and meaningfully.

Automated and Customized Content Creation

AI's potential in education extends to creating customized learning materials, including textbooks and visual aids, explicitly tailored to the needs of individual students or classes. By analyzing learning patterns, preferences, and academic performance, AI can generate textbooks focusing on areas where students need the most support or enrichment. Visual aids created by AI, such as infographics or interactive diagrams, are personalized to enhance understanding and engagement in complex topics. This bespoke approach ensures that every student receives materials that are academically appropriate and aligned with their unique learning journey, making education more effective and personalized.

Enhancing Teacher Capabilities and Roles

AI as a Collaborative Partner

As AI technology evolves, it is poised to become a valuable collaborative partner for educators, significantly enhancing various aspects of teaching. AI can assist teachers in lesson planning by suggesting content, activities, and methodologies based on their students' learning history and preferences. In student assessment, AI can provide insightful analysis of student performances, offering tailored recommendations for individual academic support. Furthermore, AI can give pedagogical recommendations, drawing from a vast pool of educational data to suggest effective teaching strategies and interventions, thereby enriching the educational experience. This collaboration between AI and educators represents a synergistic approach, where AI's data-driven insights complement the teacher's expertise and intuition.

Changing Role of Educators

AI's assumption of more administrative and basic educational tasks is expected to shift the role of educators significantly. Educators will likely move towards roles emphasizing mentorship, facilitation, and personalized guidance. With AI handling routine tasks like grading and lesson planning, teachers can dedicate more time to engaging directly with students, understanding their individual needs, and guiding their learning journeys. This shift will enable educators to focus on developing students' critical thinking, creativity, and problem-solving skills, fostering a more holistic educational experience. The integration of AI in education thus heralds a new era where the human aspects of teaching – empathy, inspiration, and personal connection – become more central than ever.

Ethical AI and Inclusive Education

Advancements in Ethical AI

The development of ethical AI frameworks is crucial to ensure equitable and unbiased access to educational resources. As AI becomes more sophisticated, there is a growing emphasis on creating AI systems that are efficient, ethically sound, and fair, which includes designing AI capable of identifying and mitigating biases in content delivery, assessment, or personalized learning paths. Ethical AI frameworks aim to ensure that all students, regardless of background, have equal access to high-quality, personalized education. The advancement in these frameworks signifies a commitment to inclusivity and fairness in educational technology, ensuring that AI enhances educational equity rather than perpetuating existing disparities.

Lifelong Learning and Continuous Education

AI in Lifelong Learning

AI is poised to play a transformative role in lifelong learning and adult education, offering a pathway for continuous education and skill development. It enables the creation of flexible and adaptive learning modules that cater to adult learners' evolving needs and schedules. AI-driven platforms can personalize content, pacing, and learning methods to suit individual preferences and professional requirements, making learning more efficient and engaging for adults. This adaptability is particularly crucial in upskilling and reskilling initiatives, where AI can swiftly align learning modules with changing job market demands. Integrating AI in adult education underscores a shift towards more personalized, accessible, and relevant learning experiences, supporting individuals in pursuing lifelong learning and career progression.

Challenges and Considerations

Addressing Challenges

Integrating AI in education brings several challenges, including data privacy, ethical considerations, and the digital divide. Data privacy concerns revolve around protecting student information, necessitating robust security measures and adherence to privacy laws. Ethical considerations involve ensuring that AI algorithms are free from biases and used in ways that benefit all students equitably. The digital divide, a significant barrier, highlights the need to ensure that AI-enhanced education is accessible to students from all socio-economic backgrounds. Addressing these challenges requires a multi-faceted approach involving policy development, technological safeguards, and a commitment to equitable access, ensuring that AI's role in education is both responsible and inclusive.

Preparing for Change

Educators, institutions, and policymakers need to prepare and adapt as the education landscape evolves with emerging AI technologies. This preparation involves continuous professional development for educators, equipping them with the necessary skills and knowledge to integrate AI tools effectively in their teaching. Institutions need to invest in infrastructure and resources to support AI integration, ensuring that these technologies are accessible to all students. Policymakers play a crucial role in shaping regulations and frameworks that guide ethical AI use in education, addressing data privacy and equity concerns. Collaborative efforts across these sectors are essential to create an education system that is responsive, equitable, and capable of harnessing the full potential of AI technologies.

Conclusion: A Future Shaped by AI

The future of AI in education holds immense promise, offering possibilities for more personalized, immersive, and inclusive learning experiences. As AI continues to evolve, it will transform how we teach and learn and redefine the role of educators and learners in this new educational landscape. Preparing for this future requires foresight, adaptability, and a commitment to leveraging AI responsibly and ethically. The upcoming chapters will guide educators and institutions in preparing for and embracing these upcoming changes in the educational landscape.

Chapter 9:
Generative AI Applications

Learning from Success: Generative AI in Practice

E xamples can help create an environment of creativity using this technology where the benefit can be brought to the educator and learner. This chapter presents a collection of examples where generative AI can be used in educational settings, offering practical applications and benefits in education. These examples provide insights into AI's practical applications and advantages in education and offer the opportunity to adapt and influence content development with new ways of thinking.

Example 1: Personalized Learning in Mathematics

Background: A high school could implement an AI-driven adaptive learning platform for its mathematics curriculum.

Implementation: The platform could use generative AI to create personalized problem sets and provide real-time feedback to students based on their performance.

Outcome: The school could measure the improvement in student engagement and understanding of complex mathematical concepts.

Example 2: AI-Enhanced Language Learning Program

Background: A language institute in another country where English is not the primary language could integrate a conversational AI chatbot to supplement its English language courses.

Implementation: The chatbot could provide students with daily conversational practice and grammar exercises, adapting to each student's learning pace.

Outcome: Students using the chatbot could demonstrate their language fluency and confidence in speaking English and review progress through language proficiency scores.

Example 3: Virtual Science Lab Simulations

Background: A university could provide a virtual science lab using AI to simulate complex experiments in chemistry and physics.

Implementation: The AI-driven simulations would allow students to conduct experiments virtually, offering a safe and cost-effective alternative to traditional labs.

Outcome: The virtual lab providing hands-on experience could result in a deeper understanding of scientific concepts; this activity could measure student performance in lab-based assessments.

Example 4: Automated Content Generation for History Courses

Background: A high school in the United States could integrate AI to generate interactive content for its history curriculum.

Implementation: The AI tool could provide dynamic timelines, infographics, and interactive quizzes based on historical events and figures.

Outcome: The interactive content could lead to higher student engagement and a deeper understanding of historical contexts measured through increased participation and discussion in history classes.

Example 5: AI-Assisted Special Education

Background: A unique education center adopts AI tools to assist students with learning disabilities.

Implementation: The AI-provided personalized learning experiences could adapt content to each student's unique needs and learning style.

Outcome: Students might demonstrate improved academic performance and engagement, with teachers using data to represent a reduction in the time spent on creating individualized learning materials.

Discussion: Lessons Learned and Best Practices

Adaptability and Customization: The success of proposed implementations and continued analysis can highlight the importance of adapting AI tools to specific educational contexts and student needs.

Teacher Involvement: Active involvement and training of educators are crucial in effectively integrating AI into the curriculum.

Continuous Evaluation: Regular assessment of the AI tools ensured they remained effective and aligned with educational goals.

Conclusion: Realizing AI's Potential in Education

These examples demonstrate the transformative possibilities of generative AI in various educational settings. They provide creative options for considering practices that can guide educators and institutions in implementing AI tools effectively. The next chapter will offer educators and educational leaders a roadmap to integrate AI into their practices, harnessing its full potential to enrich the learning experience.

Chapter 10: AI Examples

Empowering Educators with AI: Practical Guides and Examples

E xperimentation becomes an integral part of adapting to new approaches. Generative AI provides that opportunity by offering an easy-to-use solution where constraints are based on our creativity or critical thinking. This chapter provides a guide for using popular AI tools and platforms relevant to education. It includes simple examples, tool setup guidance, and best practice tips to ensure these technologies' effective and efficient use. The example below focuses on ChatGPT but could be any other large language model that emerges, such as Google's Gemini (Bard) or other solutions internationally.

Large language models have become a new competition area for many technology companies, and you should assess and choose the model that works best for you.

Example 1: Getting Started with ChatGPT for Classroom Interaction

Setting Up ChatGPT

Sign up for an OpenAI account and access ChatGPT: https://openai.com/

More details about ChatGPT can be found here: https://openai.com/blog/chatgpt

You can use ChatGPT directly via the OpenAI interface.

Basic Commands and Usage

Reference the ChatGPT guide on inputting prompts and questions, or start by simply inputting some questions at the prompt on questions you might be curious about and pressing "Enter."

Test and learn with various example questions. Building a prompt design to obtain the best output becomes an art. Try example prompts for the design of classroom discussions, quizzes, and content creation.

Best Practices

Tips on monitoring and guiding AI-generated responses for accuracy:

Table 10.1 Best Practices in Monitoring AI Accuracy

Tip Number	Monitoring and Guiding AI-Generated Responses for Accuracy
1	*Regularly Review AI Outputs*: Periodically check the responses generated by AI for accuracy and relevance, ensuring they align with educational standards and expert knowledge.
2	*Set Clear Parameters and Guidelines*: Define specific parameters and guidelines for AI-generated content, ensuring alignment with curriculum objectives and topic relevance.
3	*Implement Feedback Loops*: Establish a system for feedback from students and educators on AI responses, using this input to identify inaccuracies and areas for improvement.
4	*Utilize Cross-Verification Tools*: Employ additional tools or software for cross-verifying AI information, such as plagiarism checkers or math problem solvers.
5	*Stay Informed About AI Developments*: Keep updated on AI advancements and their educational applications to

Tip Number	Monitoring and Guiding AI-Generated Responses for Accuracy
	understand better and guide AI-generated responses. Regular training is recommended.

Example 2: Integrating AI Responses into Classroom Activities

Creating an AI-Enhanced Quiz

To design an AI-enhanced quiz, input your quiz's core topics or objectives into the AI system, specifying the subject matter and the desired difficulty level. The AI then generates a range of questions tailored to these parameters, varying from multiple-choice to short-answer formats. Each question is crafted to test specific knowledge areas, ensuring comprehensive coverage of the subject. Additionally, you can customize the AI-generated quiz by adjusting the difficulty level or focusing on sub-topics, depending on the needs of your students. The flexibility of AI in quiz creation allows for a tailored assessment experience catering to diverse learning styles and educational goals. This approach ensures that quizzes are relevant, challenging, and dynamic, keeping pace with the evolving educational content.

Example 3: Using Google AI

Introduction to Google AI Tools

Google's suite of AI tools offers a range of resources suitable for educational purposes, enhancing teaching and learning experiences. Google Colab, a notable tool in this suite, stands out for its ease of use and accessibility. It is a cloud-based platform that allows educators and students to write and execute Python code through their browsers without any setup required. This tool is particularly beneficial for computational projects, data analysis, and machine learning tasks, making advanced AI technologies accessible to students and educators with varying technical expertise. Additionally, Google AI provides extensive resources, tutorials, and documentation, making it an invaluable tool for integrating AI and machine learning concepts into the classroom.

Another Google AI product is the Gemini (Bard). It, too, is based on generative AI and should also be a part of experiencing these AI tools using similar queries to those attempted with ChatGPT.

Example 4: Creating Virtual Art Galleries with DALL-E & Similar Products

Getting Started with DALL-E

DALL-E, an AI program developed by OpenAI, is renowned for its ability to generate creative and complex images from textual descriptions. To get started, users can access DALL-E through the OpenAI website, where you can input descriptive text prompts, and the AI will generate corresponding images. The platform's user-friendly interface allows easy experimentation with different prompts to explore the AI's creative capabilities. Similar solutions to DALL-E include Google's DeepDream, which offers a unique approach to image generation using neural networks, and Adobe Sensei, a set of AI and machine learning tools that integrate with Adobe's creative software for enhancing artistic workflows. These tools open new horizons for creative expression, allowing educators, students, and artists to experiment with AI-assisted art creation.

Developing an Art Project

To create AI-generated artwork based on historical or cultural themes, begin by selecting a specific theme or era as the focus. Utilize AI tools like DALL-E or similar platforms such as Google's DeepDream and Adobe Sensei to generate artwork. Detailed input prompts are entered into these AI systems, describing the desired historical or cultural elements to produce artworks that reflect the chosen theme. To curate a virtual art gallery as a classroom project, compile the AI-generated pieces into an online gallery platform, allowing students to explore and interact digitally with the artworks. Students should be encouraged to include descriptions and analyses of their AI-generated art, fostering a deeper understanding of the historical or cultural contexts represented. These projects enhance artistic creativity and provide insightful connections between technology, art, and history.

In addition to DALL-E, Google's DeepDream offers a unique approach to generating intricate and surreal images. At the same time, Adobe Sensei integrates AI into the creative process, assisting in various aspects of digital art creation. Collectively, these tools offer diverse opportunities for exploring artistic expression through AI.

Best Practices in Using AI Tools in Education

Ensuring Ethical Use

When integrating AI tools in the classroom, it is essential to adhere to ethical and responsible use guidelines to safeguard student privacy and safety. Educators should familiarize themselves with and follow data protection laws like GDPR in Europe or FERPA in the U.S., ensuring student data collected by AI tools is used responsibly and securely and conforms to laws within countries. Maintaining transparency with students and parents about the use of AI tools and the data they collect is crucial. Educators should also be aware of potential bias in AI algorithms and actively seek tools that prioritize fairness and inclusivity. To understand current approaches and laws, continuous professional development in ethical AI use is recommended. Guidelines and resources ensure that implementing AI in classrooms enhances learning and aligns with the highest standards of ethical practice and student welfare. Also, awareness should be heightened to ensure confidential data, whether for education or business-related purposes, is not input into the models. Once input, the information can be used within the model for future queries. Understanding the models learn based on the information continually received is essential.

Fostering Human-AI Collaboration

Balancing AI tools with human teaching and interaction in the classroom involves a synergistic approach where each complements the other. Educators can use AI for data-driven insights and administrative tasks while focusing on facilitating discussions, providing mentorship, and nurturing critical thinking skills. Integrating AI as a tool that supports and enhances the learning experience rather than as a substitute for human interaction is essential. Educators should encourage students to analyze AI-generated information critically, fostering digital literacy and understanding the technology's capabilities and limitations. Incorporating activities that require students to reflect on AI's role and impact on society can also deepen their understanding. This balanced approach ensures that AI is used as a catalyst for learning and development while maintaining the essential human elements of empathy, creativity, and critical engagement in education.

Conclusion: Enhancing Education with AI

These examples and guides provide a starting point for educators to integrate AI into their teaching practices. With these tools, educators can create more engaging, personalized, and innovative learning experiences. The utilization of AI in education is continually evolving, so educators should stay informed about new developments and best practices in this exciting field. Our next chapter discusses the importance of prompt design to gain the most benefit from these tools, advancing from basic knowledge of building prompts to mastering prompt design.

Chapter 11:
Mastering Prompt Design

Developing Expertise in Prompt Design

A s we venture into this chapter, we delve into the art and science of mastering prompt design, a crucial skill for educators in advanced course development. This chapter is for those ready to elevate their course design. The journey of prompt design is not just about asking the right questions but about framing them in a way that harnesses the full potential of AI, blending creativity with precision to unlock deeper, more nuanced educational experiences.

The expertise in prompt design lies in the subtlety of language and the understanding of the AI's processing capabilities. Here, we explore the intricate dance between clarity and complexity, ensuring that prompts are understood by the AI and capable of eliciting comprehensive and contextually rich responses. This chapter will guide you through advanced techniques and strategies, such as using layered prompts, incorporating conditional statements, and leveraging the AI's ability to draw from a vast pool of knowledge. These techniques are essential for creating courses that are not just informative but are intellectually stimulating and engaging.

Moreover, this chapter will illuminate how well-crafted prompts can lead to generating content that guides us to sound content. We will examine examples where nuanced prompts have led to the development of innovative course materials, challenging assignments, and interactive learning modules. By the end of this chapter, educators will not only become adept at prompt design but also gain an appreciation for the delicate balance between guiding AI and allowing it the creative freedom to generate unique and insightful educational content.

These opening paragraphs focus on transitioning from a basic understanding to advanced mastery in prompt design for course development, emphasizing the importance of precision, creativity, and understanding AI capabilities in creating effective and engaging educational content.

The Prompt

The prompt may look ominous, but asking questions to engage and receive output is easy. Remember, verification of the information provided by generative AI is a part of the process. Generative AI can make up "hallucinations" or provide incorrect information if it does not know the answer. AI continuously learns from the information it receives in the model and the information shared.

Start by opening ChatGPT or your preferred generative AI program. Type the example prompt below in the prompt area to explore the content returned.

Prompt Design Examples

1. **Interactive Content and Lecture Development**

- How to create interactive lecture scripts and learning activities using AI.

- Example Prompt: Draft an interactive lecture script that includes educational strategies for [Course].

2. **Assignment and Project Design with AI**

- Methods to design assignments and projects.

- Example Prompt: Design a project-based assignment incorporating [specific subject and course elements].

3. **Discussion Facilitation and Collaborative Learning**

- Using AI to generate discussion questions and collaborative projects.

- Example Prompt: Suggest discussion questions for an online forum on [course].

4. Assessment and Knowledge Checks

- Creating quizzes and assessments with AI assistance.

- Example Prompt: Create a quiz focusing on the applications of business writing where the module focused on [add specific content]."

5. Incorporating Technology in Education

- Overview of digital tools and suitable for education.

- Example Prompt: Recommend digital tools that enhance learning experiences to be used in education to facilitate discussion engagement.

6. Feedback, Evaluation, and Course Improvement
- Techniques for using AI to gather and analyze student feedback.
- Example Prompt: "Draft a survey to evaluate the effectiveness of a teaching approach for [course] including open feedback questions, evaluation questions, and questions related to improvement opportunities

7. Course Objectives and Weekly Lesson Plan
  - Design the course objectives and 10-week lesson plan for a course on business writing for a Bachelor's level program.

Mastering Advanced Prompt Techniques

As we venture into the realm of advanced mastering of prompt design, we unlock a new level of sophistication and effectiveness in utilizing generative AI for educational purposes. This advanced stage of prompt design transcends basic query formulation, delving into the art of crafting prompts that provide more precision based on their request and incorporate the intricacy and foresight needed to elicit rich, context-aware responses from AI. Here, educators and course designers learn to navigate the nuances of language and AI capabilities, employing advanced techniques such as conditional phrasing, context embedding, and creative scenario-building. This mastery enables generating content that aligns with specific educational goals but is dynamically tailored to enhance student engagement and learning outcomes, marking a significant leap in the evolution of AI-assisted education.

1. **Interactive Content and Lecture Development**

   Advanced Prompt: Generate an interactive lecture script for [Subject], incorporating simulations and real-time student response analysis to enhance engagement and learning outcomes.

2. **Assignment and Project Design with AI**

   Advanced Prompt: "Design a comprehensive, multi-stage project for [Subject or Course]. The project should include a component for initial research to be conducted, development of a concept, and a final presentation where AI tools help visualize and present the findings."

3. **Discussion Facilitation and Collaborative Learning**

   Advanced Prompt: Create a series of progressively complex discussion questions for an online forum for [course name]. Include case studies or scenarios built into each question to facilitate deep, analytical discussions and collaborative problem-solving among students.

4. **Assessment and Knowledge Checks**

   Advanced Prompt: Develop a multi-layered quiz adjusting the difficulty and topics of questions based on student performance. Include a mix of question types (e.g., multiple-choice, short answer, scenario-based).

5. Incorporating Technology in Education

Advanced Prompt: Identify tools that can be used for enhanced learning experiences. Focus on tools that offer adaptive learning, predictive analytics, and immersive experiences, and provide examples of their use in a course on [Subject]."

6. Feedback, Evaluation, and Course Improvement

Advanced Prompt: Design a feedback system to evaluate the effectiveness of an educational module in [Subject]. This system should include student feedback, an engagement component, learning outcomes analysis, and asking for suggestions as part of the feedback mechanism for module improvements based on student feedback patterns.

7. Course Objectives and Weekly Lesson Plan

Advanced Prompt: Design a course [name] that incorporates the objectives and the weekly lesson plan, and incorporate details for each session on the goals and weekly course content. Incorporate the learning outcomes and weekly quizzes that enforce knowledge to be gained.

8. Workshop Modules

Advanced Prompt: Create an agenda and modules for a workshop identifying three different programs incorporating varying levels of complexity for the topic associated with [Subject]. Identify the agenda and objectives for the content, explicitly noting the content to be covered in each program and include the target audience for each level.

These advanced prompts explore deeper and more sophisticated applications leveraging technology to learning experiences. Prompt design requires imagination, creativity, and detail to enhance and ensure output addresses the request. Prompt refinement is a natural part of the process of obtaining the desired output.

Chapter 12:
Collaboration and Community Building

Fostering Collaborative Ecosystems in AI-Infused Education

T his chapter discusses how educators can actively collaborate and build communities centered around AI in education. It highlights the importance of forums, online communities, and professional networks in facilitating knowledge sharing, innovation, and support.

Building Professional Networks

Establishing AI in Education Networks

Forming networks of educators interested in AI is pivotal for fostering a collaborative and informed approach to integrating AI into education. Educators can leverage social media platforms to create and join groups to share resources, experiences, and best practices related to AI in education. Professional associations dedicated to educational technology also provide valuable networking opportunities, offering workshops, webinars, and conferences. Local meetups and interest groups can facilitate face-to-face discussions and collaborations, fostering a community of practice around AI in education. Encouraging interdisciplinary collaboration is crucial, bringing together educators from various subject areas to develop a holistic approach to AI integration. This interdisciplinary exchange enriches the understanding and application of AI, ensuring it is used effectively across different educational contexts. These networks act not just as forums for sharing knowledge but also as support systems, driving innovation and excellence in the use of AI in education.

Participating in Professional Development Workshops and Conferences

Attending professional development workshops and conferences focused on AI in education is essential for educators to stay updated and connected. These forums offer unique networking opportunities, enabling educators to build relationships with peers, industry experts, and researchers. Participation in such events also facilitates the exchange of ideas, collaboration on projects, and discussion of challenges and solutions in implementing AI in educational settings. Moreover, workshops and conferences often provide hands-on experiences with new tools and technologies, enhancing educators' skills and confidence in integrating AI into their curriculum. Attending these events is a proactive step for educators to remain at the forefront of educational innovation and bring valuable insights and practices to their institutions or work.

Engaging with Industry Experts

Collaboration with AI industry experts and technologists is vital for educators to gain practical insights and access to advanced resources in AI education. Engaging with professionals from the AI field provides an opportunity to understand the latest trends, tools, and real-world applications of AI, which can be invaluable in shaping effective educational strategies. Such collaborations can lead to sharing resources like cutting-edge software, datasets, and case studies, enhancing the quality of AI education. Industry experts can also offer guest lectures or workshops, providing students and educators with firsthand insights into the practical challenges and opportunities in the field of AI. This partnership between education and industry bridges the gap between theoretical learning and practical application, ensuring that the AI curriculum remains relevant and impactful. Furthermore, these connections can open avenues for research collaborations, internships, and student project-based learning opportunities, fostering a more dynamic and experiential learning environment.

Utilizing Online Platforms and Forums

Online Forums and Discussion Boards

Online forums and discussion boards, such as LinkedIn groups dedicated to AI in education, are invaluable educational resources. These platforms provide a space for sharing experiences, challenges, and solutions, fostering a community of practice among educators at different stages of AI integration. Navigating and contributing to these forums allows educators to stay informed about the latest developments, teaching strategies, and technological advancements in AI education. They also serve as a supportive network where educators can seek advice, offer guidance, and exchange ideas with peers with similar interests and challenges. Participation in these online communities encourages collaborative learning and knowledge sharing, essential for AI's effective implementation and evolution in educational settings. Engaging in these forums enriches the individual educator's experience and contributes to the broader academic community's understanding and application of AI.

Collaborative Learning Management Systems (LMS)

Collaborative Learning Management Systems (LMS) involve using AI-integrated LMS platforms for collaborative teaching, resource sharing, and engaging in professional discussions.

Example: Canvas LMS with AI plugins for collaborative teaching.

Creating Open-Source Educational Resources

AI-integrated Learning Management Systems (LMS) like Canvas with AI plugins are revolutionizing the landscape of collaborative teaching and resource sharing. These platforms enable educators to personalize learning experiences, automate administrative tasks, and facilitate effective resource distribution. AI integration in LMS platforms can enhance the collaborative teaching experience by offering predictive insights on student performance, suggesting content adaptations, and fostering more interactive and engaging learning environments. For example, AI plugins in Canvas can analyze student participation and progress, allowing educators to tailor their teaching strategies collaboratively in real time. These platforms also serve as a hub for professional discussions, where educators can share best practices, pedagogical innovations, and insights gained from AI analytics. AI-integrated LMS platforms like Canvas streamline administrative processes and enrich the teaching and learning experience, fostering a more connected and efficient educational community.

Developing Collaborative Research and Projects

Joint Research Initiatives

Joint research initiatives in AI education are vital for advancing the field and fostering innovation. These initiatives drive collaborative research on AI applications in education by forming partnerships between educational institutions, tech companies, and researchers. These collaborations often result in valuable contributions to academic journals and publications, sharing new findings and insights with the broader educational community. Furthermore, joint initiatives frequently involve collaborating on grants and funding opportunities, which are crucial for supporting in-depth research and development in AI education. Such partnerships pool diverse expertise and resources and open avenues for practical application and validation of research findings. These collaborations ultimately contribute to a deeper understanding of AI's potential in education and pave the way for innovative educational tools and methodologies informed by cutting-edge research.

Student Involvement in AI Projects

Involving students in AI-related projects is a dynamic way to bridge the gap between theoretical learning and practical application. Such involvement encourages active collaboration between educators, students, and the tech industry, providing students with hands-on experience and real-world insights. Initiatives like student-led AI workshops and hackathons are practical platforms for students to apply their AI knowledge, fostering innovation and problem-solving skills. These events also offer opportunities for networking with professionals and peers, giving students a glimpse into the tech industry and potential career paths. Engaging students in these projects enhances their understanding of AI and cultivates essential skills like teamwork, creativity, and technical proficiency. These experiences are instrumental in preparing students for the rapidly evolving tech landscape and encouraging them to become active contributors to the field of AI.

Community Engagement and Outreach

Public Education and Outreach Programs

Public education and outreach programs are crucial in raising awareness and understanding of AI in education among the broader public. Organizing such programs involves reaching out to communities through workshops, seminars, and informational sessions that demystify AI technologies and their impact on education. These initiatives are often most effective in partnership with local schools and community centers, ensuring accessibility and relevance to diverse audiences. The goal is to promote digital literacy and an understanding of AI, empowering individuals with knowledge about how AI shapes the educational landscape. These programs also serve to address common misconceptions and fears surrounding AI, fostering a more informed and positive perspective on the potential benefits of AI in education. By engaging the wider community, these outreach programs contribute to building a society better equipped to adapt to and benefit from the advancements in AI and technology.

Policy Advocacy and Consultation

Collaboration with policymakers is essential to advocate for AI's responsible and ethical use in education. Educators and AI experts must engage in dialogue with policymakers to shape policies that govern the use of AI in educational settings, ensuring they promote equity, privacy, and effectiveness. Participation in consultations, panels, and policy-making forums allows educators to provide insights and recommendations based on their firsthand experience with AI in the classroom. These interactions influence AI education policy, ensuring it aligns with educational needs and ethical standards. Such collaborations also help establish guidelines and frameworks that safeguard against biases and misuse of AI in education while fostering an environment conducive to innovation and learning. Educators and AI professionals can help shape a policy landscape that supports AI's positive and ethical integration into education systems by actively participating in these discussions.

Conclusion: A United Journey in AI Education

Building a collaborative and supportive community is vital to successfully integrating AI into education. By sharing knowledge, resources, and experiences, educators can navigate the complexities of AI, innovate in their teaching practices, and contribute to developing an ethically informed, technologically advanced educational landscape.

Chapter 13:
Legal and Regulatory
Framework

Navigating the Legal Landscape of AI in Education

T his chapter outlines the essential legal and regulatory considerations that educators and educational leaders should know when implementing AI in the classroom. It emphasizes the importance of understanding and complying with laws and regulations to ensure responsible and ethical use of AI in educational settings.

Understanding Data Privacy Laws

Family Educational Rights and Privacy Act (FERPA)

The Family Educational Rights and Privacy Act (FERPA) is a critical U.S. federal law that plays a pivotal role in protecting the privacy of student education records. FERPA grants parents and students certain rights regarding access to and the confidentiality of educational records, including the right to review these records and request corrections. It also provides guidelines on who can access such information and under what circumstances.

Understanding and complying with FERPA is essential for AI systems processing educational data. AI tools need to be designed to safeguard student data, ensuring that academic record collection, storage, and analysis adhere to FERPA regulations. Implementing robust security measures can aid in preventing unauthorized access and ensure that data sharing aligns with the consent provisions outlined by FERPA.

Educational institutions utilizing AI must also be transparent about how these tools use student data, providing clarity to students and parents about their rights under FERPA. AI developers must work with the education sector and legal experts to ensure their technologies meet FERPA standards. This compliance protects students' privacy and builds trust in using AI within educational settings.

General Data Protection Regulation (GDPR)

The General Data Protection Regulation (GDPR) is a crucial framework in the EU for protecting personal data, significantly impacting educational institutions and AI tools handling EU students' data. GDPR mandates explicit consent for data collection and guarantees individuals' rights over personal information, including access, correction, and deletion. AI systems in education must ensure compliance with GDPR by adopting transparent data practices and safeguarding the confidentiality and integrity of student data. Educational institutions using AI tools must implement 'privacy by design' and conduct regular risk assessments to align with GDPR. Additionally, appointing a Data Protection Officer (DPO) is essential for overseeing data protection strategies and maintaining GDPR compliance. Adherence to these regulations is vital for legal compliance and trust in educational AI applications.

Children's Online Privacy Protection Act (COPPA)

The Children's Online Privacy Protection Act (COPPA) sets strict regulations on collecting personal information from children under the age of 13. This U.S. federal law requires parental consent to collect, use, or disclose a child's personal information by online services, including educational AI tools. Therefore, AI applications in education must have robust mechanisms to verify age and obtain parental consent before collecting data from children. These tools should also provide transparent information about their data practices, ensuring transparency and adherence to COPPA's privacy protections. Understanding and complying with COPPA is crucial for educators and institutions implementing AI tools to protect children's privacy and maintain a safe online educational environment. Compliance ensures that young learners benefit from AI-driven education while safeguarding their personal information.

Bias and Discrimination in AI

Algorithmic Fairness and Non-Discrimination

Bias and discrimination in AI, particularly in educational applications, raise significant legal and ethical concerns. If not carefully designed and monitored, AI algorithms can perpetuate and amplify existing biases, leading to unfair and discriminatory student outcomes. Developers and educators must prioritize algorithmic fairness and non-discrimination, ensuring that AI systems are equitable and unbiased. On-going monitoring needs to occur, including regularly auditing AI tools for potential biases and implementing diverse datasets to train these systems. Legal implications of biased AI include violations of anti-discrimination laws and can lead to a loss of trust in educational technologies. Ensuring fairness in AI systems is not only a legal imperative but also essential to uphold the principles of equity and justice in educational settings.

Best Practices for Mitigating Bias

Mitigating bias in AI applications requires ongoing review and implementation of best practices focused on auditing and testing AI tools. Regular and thorough audits of AI algorithms should be conducted to identify and address any inherent biases. Scrutinizing the data sets used for AI training is essential to understanding bias; the data set needs to be diverse and representative of different populations. Involving multidisciplinary teams in the development and review process can provide varied perspectives, helping to identify potential biases that might not be evident initially. Testing AI tools in natural educational settings and gathering feedback from diverse users is also crucial. These strategies help ensure that AI applications in education are equitable and inclusive, providing fair and unbiased learning experiences for all students.

Intellectual Property and Copyright Considerations

Copyright Laws and AI-Generated Content

Various copyright laws are under review to determine the impacts as AI moves forward. The following represents a few considerations as AI is used, including copyright issues related to AI-generated materials, such as text, images, and code.

Consider seeking legal support to advise on using and sharing AI-generated educational content in the following areas:

- Licensing and Use of AI Software
- Accessibility and Inclusivity
- Creating Inclusive AI-driven Learning Environments
- Cybersecurity and Protection
- Cybersecurity Laws and Regulations

Conclusion: Legal Responsibility in AI Usage

Educators and educational leaders must navigate a complex legal landscape when implementing AI in the classroom. Understanding and adhering to these legal and regulatory considerations is crucial for responsible and ethical AI deployment in education. Continuous education and consultation with legal experts are essential as laws and technologies evolve.

Chapter 14:
Business Writing Course
Content Creation

Utilizing Generative AI for Course Development

T his chapter focuses on how AI can revolutionize the design and delivery of a college-level business writing course. It demonstrates the use of AI in defining course objectives, designing educational modules, and creating quizzes. AI's role in this context includes generating comprehensive overviews, developing content for specific modules, and formulating assessment questions. The integration of AI streamlines the course development process, ensuring that the content is relevant, engaging, and tailored to the learning outcomes. It also highlights AI's ability to adapt content based on real-time feedback, enhancing the overall learning experience.

Course Overview

The course was designed with AI assistance based on the prompt to design a course based on the title. It was then asked to build out the course description, the target audience, the course objective, and each module. The detail provides what is typically found in a course design. For this example, AI offered a business writing course description covering fundamental principles, historical context, and modern practices. It includes interactive modules, each focusing on different aspects of business communication, such as writing formats, ethical considerations, and evolving trends, with additional prompts provided to build out each module.

Course Title

"Mastering Business Writing: Communicating Effectively in the Corporate World"

Course Description

This course offers a comprehensive guide to effective business writing tailored for today's dynamic corporate environment. It covers various forms of business communication, from traditional reports and proposals to digital-age correspondences. Students will learn the nuances of tone, style, and format appropriate for diverse business contexts. The course also addresses the ethical aspects of business communication and explores the latest trends influencing corporate writing.

Target Audience

The course is designed for aspiring business professionals, corporate employees, and entrepreneurs who aim to enhance their written communication skills. It is also suitable for students in business-related academic programs seeking practical insights into corporate communication.

Course Objective

This course will equip participants with the skills and knowledge required for proficient business writing. It seeks to foster an understanding of effective communication strategies, adaptability in various writing formats, and a keen awareness of ethical considerations in a business setting. The course strives to enhance student's ability to communicate ideas persuasively and professionally in business.

Module Design Using Generative AI

Module 1: Basics of Business Writing

- AI Contribution: Generate an introductory overview of business writing essentials and concepts.

- Quiz: AI-created multiple-choice questions on fundamental principles of business writing.

Module 2: Evolution of Business Communication

- AI Contribution: Compile a brief history of business communication and its evolution.
- Quiz: True/False questions focusing on historical changes and developments.

Module 3: Business Writing Formats

- AI Contribution: Develop detailed guides on various business writing formats (e.g., emails, reports, proposals).
- Quiz: Short answer questions testing knowledge of different formats and their appropriate use.

Module 4: Effective Business Communication

- AI Contribution: Curate examples and case studies on effective business communication strategies.
- Quiz: Case study analysis questions evaluating communication effectiveness.

Module 5: Ethical Considerations in Business Writing

- AI Contribution: Generate content on ethical considerations, such as confidentiality and transparency in business writing.
- Quiz: Scenario-based questions on ethical dilemmas in business communication.

Module 6: Tone and Style in Business Writing

- AI Contribution: Create content exploring the importance of tone and style tailored to various business contexts.
- Quiz: Questions assessing understanding of appropriate tone and style for different business scenarios.

Module 7: Modern Trends in Business Writing

- AI Contribution: Discuss current trends in business writing, including the impact of digital media.
- Quiz: Predictive analysis-based questions on the evolution of business writing trends.

Module 8: Critical Writing and Analysis

- AI Contribution: Offer guidance on developing critical writing and analysis skills in a business context.
- Quiz: Essay questions encouraging critical thinking and application of business writing principles.

This module design for a business writing course offers a structured and comprehensive approach, leveraging AI for content creation and assessment while covering essential aspects of business communication from basics to advanced analysis.

Best Practices for Using Generative AI in Course Development

Human Oversight: Ensure human review and refinement of AI-generated content for accuracy and relevance.

Balanced Approach: Combine AI-generated content with traditional teaching resources for a comprehensive learning experience.

Continuous Update: Utilize AI to regularly update course content, keeping it current with the latest developments in the field.

Conclusion: AI as a Tool for Educational Innovation

This example illustrates how generative AI can significantly aid in developing a comprehensive and dynamic course. Educators can create engaging, up-to-date, personalized educational experiences by leveraging AI.

Chapter 15:
Skill Sets for Using Generative AI in Education

Navigating the Complexities of Generative AI

Without a doubt, educators and educational leaders face many challenges and opportunities in this new world of AI. Understanding the challenges of using generative AI in educational settings becomes imperative to protect individuals and organizations. Please also refer back to Chapter 13:
Legal and Regulatory Framework. It also outlines employees' essential skill sets to utilize these tools effectively.

Challenges in Using Generative AI

Data Privacy and Security Concerns

When utilizing AI tools that process student data, it is crucial to address data privacy and security concerns vigilantly, ensuring strict compliance with GDPR and FERPA regulations designed to protect personal and educational information. Educators and institutions must implement robust security measures, maintain transparency in data usage, and ensure ethical handling of student data to prevent breaches and unauthorized access.

Bias and Fairness in AI Models

It is essential to recognize that biases can be inadvertently embedded in AI algorithms, potentially leading to unfair or discriminatory educational content and assessment outcomes. Ensuring fairness in AI models requires proactive measures such as diverse data training, regular bias audits, and involving multidisciplinary teams in the AI development process. These steps help to minimize biases, promoting equitable and just applications of AI in education.

Reliability and Accuracy

Concerns about the reliability and accuracy of AI-generated content underscore the need for continuous verification and validation processes. It is vital to ensure that AI systems in education are regularly audited and updated to maintain high standards of accuracy. Educators should also be equipped to critically assess AI-generated content, ensuring its alignment with educational objectives and factual correctness.

Integration with Existing Systems

Integrating AI tools into existing educational technologies and infrastructures presents technical challenges that require careful planning and execution. It is crucial to ensure compatibility between AI systems and existing digital platforms, with a focus on seamless data exchange and user experience. The strategy should minimize disruption to current systems while maximizing the benefits of AI enhancements.

Keeping Pace with Rapid Technological Changes

Educators and educational institutions face the challenge of staying abreast of the rapidly evolving landscape of AI technologies and their applications in education. Continuous professional development and active engagement with technological communities are essential to keep pace with these changes. Educational practices are to remain relevant through the use of emerging AI capabilities.

Skill Sets Required for Utilizing Generative AI

Technical Proficiency

Developing a basic understanding of AI and machine learning concepts is crucial for educators and students in the modern educational landscape. Familiarity with various AI tools and platforms and the ability to effectively navigate and utilize these technologies is essential for leveraging their full potential in educational settings. This proficiency enhances teaching and learning experiences and prepares students and educators for a technology-driven future.

Data Literacy

Data literacy, encompassing the skills to understand and interpret data, is increasingly crucial in an educational environment where AI systems are prevalent. For educators and students, proficiency in data literacy means critically analyzing and making informed decisions based on AI tools' data-driven content and insights. This skill set is essential not only for the effective use of AI in education but also for fostering a deeper understanding of how AI algorithms function and impact learning outcomes.

Critical Thinking and Problem-Solving

Critical thinking and problem-solving skills are essential when interacting with AI-generated content and outcomes. Educators and students must be adept at assessing the validity and relevance of AI-provided information and identifying any potential biases or inaccuracies. This skill set enables them to question and critique AI outputs and develop practical solutions and approaches for utilizing AI in an educational context. These competencies ensure responsible and informed use of AI tools in learning environments.

Ethical and Legal Awareness

In the context of AI in education, it is crucial to understand the ethical implications and legal considerations deeply. Awareness of issues related to privacy, data security, and intellectual property are avenues to build knowledge. Educators and institutions must navigate these aspects responsibly, ensuring compliance with relevant laws and upholding ethical standards in deploying and using AI technologies.

Adaptability and Continuous Learning

Adaptability and a commitment to continuous learning are essential in the rapidly evolving field of AI in education. Educators and institutions need to be open to regularly updating their knowledge and skills to keep pace with new AI technologies and methodologies. This willingness to learn and adapt is essential for effectively integrating emerging AI tools into educational practices. Staying current with technological advancements ensures educators can leverage the most effective and innovative AI applications to enhance teaching and learning experiences.

Conclusion: Preparing for a Future with AI

General knowledge and AI principles become essential to understand as AI becomes mainstream in educational technology. Understanding the challenges and developing the necessary skill sets are crucial steps for educators and educational institutions in harnessing the potential of generative AI. The education community can effectively leverage AI technologies to enhance teaching and learning experiences by addressing these challenges and fostering these skills.

Chapter 16:
Possibilities of Generative AI in Education

Exploring the Horizon of AI Innovations

I mmersing ourselves into using AI can help us understand the nuances and benefits of these tools. Insights and benefits will continue to emerge as the potential new features and functionalities of generative AI emerge in the next several years. The expectation is that advancements will further revolutionize the educational landscape.

Anticipated Advancements in Generative AI

Enhanced Personalization and Adaptability

Future advancements in generative AI are expected to significantly enhance the personalization and adaptability of learning experiences. AI systems will likely be capable of tailoring content and teaching approaches to individual students' unique learning styles, preferences, and progress levels. This evolution will facilitate a more intuitive and responsive educational environment where each student's learning journey becomes a journey through technology. These advancements promise to make education more effective, engaging, and aligned with each learner's needs and goals.

Real-Time Language Translation and Interpretation

Natural language processing (NLP) advancements are poised to revolutionize education through real-time translation and interpretation capabilities. This technological progression will enable educational content to become universally accessible, breaking down language barriers that traditionally limit learning opportunities. Students and educators from diverse linguistic backgrounds can interact and access resources in their preferred languages, fostering a more inclusive and global educational environment. Integrating real-time translation and interpretation in educational tools will significantly enhance all participants' communication, collaboration, and learning experiences.

Advanced Predictive Analytics

More significantly, sophisticated predictive analytics will bring about the continued advancement of AI in education. These enhanced capabilities will enable educators to proactively address individual student needs, customize learning paths, and improve educational strategies. This predictive power of AI will be instrumental in shaping a more responsive and effective educational environment.

Emerging Functionalities in AI Tools

Immersive and Interactive Learning Environments

Emerging functionalities in AI tools, particularly the integration of virtual and augmented reality (VR/AR), are set to transform educational experiences by creating highly immersive and interactive learning environments. These technologies will enable students to engage with lifelike simulations of real-world scenarios and historical events, enhancing their understanding and engagement with the subject matter. This immersion promises to make learning more dynamic and experiential, bridging the gap between theoretical knowledge and practical application.

Automated Curriculum Design and Updating

Advancements in AI offer the potential for systems that can autonomously design and continually update curricula. These AI systems could adapt educational content to align with the latest standards, research findings, and student feedback, ensuring the curriculum remains current and relevant. This automation promises to enhance the efficiency and responsiveness of educational programming, allowing educators to focus more on teaching and less on administrative tasks. Integrating AI in curriculum design and updating represents a significant step towards a more dynamic and adaptive educational landscape.

Intelligent Tutoring Systems

The development of advanced AI tutors marks a significant evolution in educational technology. These intelligent systems are envisioned to extend beyond academic support, offering personalized guidance on study habits, time management, and mental well-being. Their ability to adapt to individual student needs and learning styles will provide a more holistic educational support system. This progression in AI tutoring reflects an integrated approach to education, addressing student development's academic and personal aspects.

New Features in Content Creation and Assessment

Dynamic Content Generation

The advancement of AI in education is increasingly enabling the generation of dynamic and interactive content tailored to enhance the learning experience. AI tools can now create simulations, educational games, and quizzes that respond and adapt in real-time to student interactions. This dynamic content generation allows for a more personalized learning experience, where the difficulty level and nature of the content can adjust based on the student's performance and engagement. Such AI-driven content makes learning more engaging and ensures the educational material is relevant and challenging for each learner. Incorporating these adaptive learning tools represents a shift towards more responsive and student-centric education, where content evolves to meet each student's unique needs and pace. This approach not only aids in maintaining student interest but also significantly enhances the effectiveness of the learning process.

Automated and Fair Assessment Tools

Emerging AI technologies are poised to revolutionize assessment in education with tools capable of providing fair and unbiased evaluations of student work. These sophisticated AI systems are designed to assess a wide range of student submissions, from essays to complex problem-solving tasks, ensuring consistency and objectivity in grading. The development of these tools focuses on eliminating human biases and providing equitable evaluations for all students. By leveraging advanced algorithms, AI assessment tools can accurately gauge student understanding and performance, contributing to a more effective and just educational system. Ensuring fairness in these automated tools is crucial for maintaining trust and credibility in AI-assisted assessments.

Collaborative AI Learning Platforms

Collaborative AI learning platforms represent a significant advancement in educational technology designed to facilitate interactive group learning experiences. These platforms are tools for individual student assistance and are engineered to foster group interactions, discussions, and collaborative projects. By integrating AI, these platforms can enhance group dynamics, suggest collaborative tasks based on group skills and interests, and provide real-time assistance during group activities. This approach leverages AI's capabilities to support individual learning and enrich the collaborative educational experience, encouraging teamwork and collective problem-solving.

Ethical and Inclusive AI Development

Focus on Ethical AI

A key focus in developing AI systems for education is prioritizing ethical considerations, inclusivity, and accessibility. It is essential to design equitable AI tools that cater to a diverse student population, including those with disabilities. This commitment to ethical AI involves creating systems free from biases that uphold the principles of fairness and justice in educational settings.

Ensuring that AI tools are inclusive and accessible aligns with ethical standards and enhances AI's overall effectiveness and impact in education.

AI Literacy and Digital Citizenship

Incorporating AI literacy into educational curricula is becoming increasingly important, teaching students how to interact responsibly and effectively with AI technologies. This includes understanding the functionalities and limitations of AI and ethical considerations and best practices in using these tools. Developing AI literacy prepares students to navigate a tech-driven world and fosters responsible digital citizenship. It empowers students with the knowledge and skills to critically assess and utilize AI technologies, ensuring they are well-equipped for future challenges and opportunities in the digital landscape.

Preparing for the Future

Continuous Professional Development

Educators need to engage in continuous professional development in the context of rapidly advancing AI technologies. Staying updated with the latest AI advancements and educational applications is crucial for effectively integrating these technologies into teaching practices. This ongoing learning process ensures that educators can utilize AI tools to their fullest potential and helps them guide their students in navigating an AI-enhanced educational landscape. Emphasizing continuous professional development is vital to preparing educators and students for a future where AI plays a significant role in education and beyond.

Policy and Infrastructure Adaptation

Educational policymakers and institutions must adapt infrastructures and policies to effectively accommodate and regulate emerging AI technologies. Updating educational frameworks to integrate AI tools, ensuring data privacy, and establishing guidelines for ethical AI use in educational settings are several components to consider. Such adaptations are crucial for creating an environment conducive to leveraging AI's potential while safeguarding standards and student well-being.

Conclusion: A Future Shaped by AI in Education

The future of education is poised for transformative changes driven by advancements in AI technology. AI promises to redefine educational delivery and experiences, offering unprecedented personalization, efficiency, and engagement. For educators and leaders, staying informed and adaptable to these advancements is crucial. By embracing AI's potential and preparing for its integration, they can ensure that the educational landscape evolves to maximize learning outcomes and enrich student experiences. The journey towards an AI-integrated future in education is an opportunity to reshape learning for the better, making it more inclusive, effective, and aligned with the needs of a rapidly changing world.

Chapter 17:
Enhancing Engagement and
Recall in Courses

Strategies for Interactive and Memorable Learning Experiences

S tudent learning and recall are paramount in a classroom, e-learning or workshop setting. Creating engagement and learning opportunities benefits the goal of retention. For many students, the application of learning to real-world examples is the trigger to understanding. Here are several practical strategies for designing course interactions and techniques to enhance learning recall.

Creating Engagement in Courses

Interactive Content and Activities

To enhance engagement in courses, integrating a variety of interactive content is essential. Using quizzes and polls during lessons actively involves students and provides immediate feedback on their comprehension. Additionally, interactive videos that allow students to make decisions or engage in virtual simulations further deepen their engagement and understanding.

Equally important is the implementation of hands-on activities. For example, students could develop a marketing plan for a hypothetical product in a business course, applying class-taught concepts. Similarly, in a science course, virtual lab experiments replicating real-world scenarios can offer practical applications of theoretical knowledge. These interactive and practical methods keep students interested and solidify the link between academic learning and its application in real-world contexts.

Collaborative Learning Approaches

Fostering group discussions, peer reviews, and collaborative projects encourages active participation. As an example, in the business writing course example, promoting collaborative learning approaches is crucial for enhancing student participation and engagement. Encouraging group discussions is one effective method; for instance, students can engage in debates or analyze case studies related to business communication challenges. Developing and promoting critical thinking and problem-solving skills can be designed into the experience for learners.

Implementing peer reviews is another valuable approach. Students could be assigned to review and provide feedback on each other's business proposals or reports. This process helps students learn from their peers and sharpens their editing and analytical skills, essential for effective business writing. Peer reviews often bring good results; some students respond to their peer group by listening to constructive comments.

Collaborative projects are particularly impactful in a business writing context. Students could work in teams to create a comprehensive communication strategy for a simulated company or develop a series of business documents for a mock product launch. These projects simulate real-world business scenarios, encouraging teamwork and the practical application of writing skills. By incorporating these collaborative learning approaches, business writing courses can become more dynamic, interactive, and reflective of real-world business communication environments.

Gamification Techniques

Integrating gamification techniques into business writing courses can significantly enhance the learning experience by making it more engaging and enjoyable. Incorporating elements like point scoring, competitions, and rewards adds a playful, competitive edge to the learning process.

One example based on our business course could be a 'Business Communication Challenge,' where students accumulate points for effectively drafting various business documents, such as emails, proposals, or press releases. Points could be awarded based on clarity, creativity, and adherence to business writing standards, with the top scorers receiving recognition or rewards.

Another example is a 'Pitch Perfect' competition, where students develop and present business pitches or proposals. This activity can be gamified by having peer voting or a panel of judges to score each presentation based on specific criteria, such as persuasiveness, clarity, and originality.

Award winners' bonus points or privileges can apply to leading the following class discussion or choosing a topic for future assignments, which are examples of effective use of awards.

These gamification techniques make learning more interactive and closely mirror real-world business scenarios, preparing students for professional communication challenges in a fun and engaging manner.

Designing Course Interactions

Utilizing Technology for Interaction

Incorporating educational technology tools can significantly elevate student interaction and engagement. Tools like virtual whiteboards, online discussion forums, and breakout rooms in virtual classrooms offer diverse ways to enhance the learning experience.

One practical application, for example, in our business writing course could involve using virtual whiteboards during live sessions for collaborative editing exercises. Students can work together in real-time to refine and improve a sample business document, such as a press release or a project proposal, fostering teamwork and enhancing editing skills.

Utilize breakout rooms for role-play activities by dividing students into small groups, each tasked with negotiating a business deal or resolving a conflict through written communication. This setup simulates real-life business scenarios and encourages students to practice and refine their business writing and communication strategies in a controlled, collaborative environment.

Additionally, use online discussion forums for weekly reflective exercises, where students post their analyses of different business communication styles or share experiences of applying course learnings in real-world situations. This continuous interaction outside class hours promotes more profound engagement with course concepts and fosters a community learning atmosphere.

By employing these technological tools, business writing courses can offer more dynamic and practical interactions, closely mirroring real-world business communication contexts and enhancing the overall educational value.

Personalized Feedback Mechanisms

Incorporating personalized feedback mechanisms in business writing courses can significantly enhance student learning. Utilizing AI-driven tools or crafting personalized messages allows for targeted guidance tailored to each student's progress and needs.

For example, in a business writing course, an AI-driven tool could analyze student submissions of a business proposal or report. It could provide individualized tone, structure, grammar, and business terminology feedback. This AI-generated feedback would highlight areas needing improvement and offer suggestions for enhancement, ensuring each student receives specific, actionable advice to refine their writing skills. Such personalized feedback is invaluable for students to understand their strengths and areas for growth, fostering a more tailored and practical learning experience.

Role-Playing and Simulations

Incorporate role-playing scenarios and simulations that mimic real-life situations, allowing students to apply their knowledge in a controlled environment.

For example, in our business writing course, students could take on the roles of different stakeholders in a company, such as marketing directors or project managers, and be tasked with drafting various business communications pertinent to their assigned role, like client proposals, interdepartmental emails, or press releases. This activity helps students practice writing in diverse business contexts and enhances their understanding of how effective communication varies across different roles and scenarios. Such practical exercises encourage the application of theoretical knowledge in lifelike settings, enriching the overall learning experience.

Increasing Learning Recall

Repetition and Spaced Learning

Incorporating spaced repetition into the design of business writing courses can significantly enhance memory and recall of concepts. This technique involves revisiting crucial topics at intervals throughout the course.

For example, in our business writing course, fundamental principles of effective business communication introduced early in the course can be periodically reviewed and applied in subsequent modules.

Students might start by learning to craft professional emails and revisit these concepts when working on a comprehensive business proposal. Reviewing earlier concepts in this manner ensures continuous reinforcement of lessons, aiding in long-term retention and a deeper understanding of the course material.

Mnemonic Devices and Storytelling

Utilizing mnemonic devices and storytelling techniques can make learning in business writing courses more engaging and memorable.

For example, to teach the elements of effective business communication, an instructor might use the mnemonic device "CLEAR" (Concise, logical, engaging, accurate, and relevant). Each letter represents a crucial component of good business writing. Alongside this, the instructor could use storytelling by creating a narrative around a successful business leader who excels in communication, illustrating how each element of "CLEAR" is applied in real-life scenarios. This method helps students easily recall the fundamentals of business writing and understand their practical application in a memorable, relatable context.

Active Learning Techniques

Active learning techniques involve students actively engaging through discussions, peer teaching, and applying knowledge in practical scenarios.

For instance, for the business writing course, students could participate in a workshop to revise and improve a sample business document. They would first discuss in groups to identify areas for enhancement, then apply their writing skills to refine the document, and finally, present their revisions to the class. This exercise encourages active participation in problem-solving and facilitates peer-to-peer learning and practical application of business writing principles. Such activities make the learning process more interactive and reinforce the valuable utility of course content.

Leveraging AI and Data Analytics

AI-Powered Adaptive Learning

Utilize AI to create adaptive learning paths for students, adjusting the course content based on their progress and performance.

For example, related to the business writing course developed, the AI system could analyze a student's performance on initial writing assignments and quizzes, identifying specific areas such as tone, clarity, or business terminology that need improvement. Based on this analysis, the AI could recommend targeted exercises or additional reading materials to the student. This personalized approach ensures that each student receives the most relevant and beneficial instruction, facilitating a more efficient and effective learning experience. By leveraging AI in this way, business writing courses can cater to the unique learning needs of each student, enhancing their overall mastery of the subject.

Data-Driven Insights for Course Improvement

Utilizing data analytics in business writing courses offers valuable insights into student engagement and performance, enabling continual refinement of course content and delivery methods.

Instructors can analyze data gathered from student interactions with online course materials, such as time spent on specific modules or assessment performance trends, to identify areas where students excel or struggle. They can use this information to adjust the course pacing, introduce supplementary materials, or restructure modules for clarity and effectiveness. This data-driven approach enables informed decisions, enhancing the quality and effectiveness of the business writing course to meet students' evolving needs.

Conclusion: Building a More Engaging and Retentive Learning Environment

By adopting these strategies, educators can create courses and workshops that are engaging and conducive to long-term learning and recall. It is about creating an environment where learning is an active, enjoyable, and continuous process.

Chapter 18:
Performance Metrics

P erformance metrics are essential for assessing course content development, student engagement, and the quality of interactions in educational settings. These metrics are vital tools for educators and learning community leaders, providing data-driven insights to evaluate and refine teaching strategies effectively.

Metrics for Course Content Development

Alignment with Learning Objectives

The course content should be evaluated against the learning objectives, which involves reviewing assessment results to determine if students meet the targeted outcomes and identifying gaps between what is taught and the intended learning goals. This process helps to align the course material with the desired educational results, ensuring that each aspect of the curriculum contributes effectively to the overall learning objectives. Regularly adjusting the course content based on this evaluation can improve educational outcomes and a more focused learning experience for students.

Content Comprehensiveness and Accuracy

Assess the course material's breadth, depth, accuracy, and clarity, including conducting peer reviews or expert consultations to ensure the content's comprehensiveness and correctness. This assessment is crucial for maintaining high-quality educational standards and ensuring the information presented is reliable and transparent. Regular updates and revisions based on these evaluations can significantly enhance the course's effectiveness and relevance to current academic and industry standards.

Up-to-date and Relevant Material

Regularly review the course material to ensure it incorporates the latest findings, theories, and practices relevant to the subject, potentially involving integrating recent case studies or industry trends to keep the course current. Staying updated with contemporary developments and real-world applications enhances the course's relevance and practicality. This approach ensures that students learn the most current information and skills, preparing them effectively for real-world challenges and opportunities in their field.

Multimedia and Interactive Elements

Monitor the effectiveness of multimedia (videos, audio, animations) and interactive elements (quizzes, simulations) in engaging students and enhancing the learning process. Feedback from students can be a valuable source of information on how these elements contribute to their understanding of the course material.

Metrics for Assessing Student Engagement

Participation Rates

Assess student participation by tracking their involvement in discussions, interactive activities, and completion of assignments, as this indicates their engagement with the course material. Active participation often reflects a deeper understanding and interest in the subject, making it a crucial metric for gauging the effectiveness of teaching methods and the resonance of course content with students.

High participation rates often correlate with greater interest and engagement in the course.

Completion Rates

Monitoring the rates at which students complete courses, individual modules, or specific activities can strongly indicate their commitment and engagement. High completion rates suggest the course material is engaging and students are motivated to complete the learning journey.

Feedback and Surveys

Gathering and analyzing student feedback through surveys and course evaluations is essential. This feedback provides direct insights into students' perceptions of engagement and satisfaction, helping educators identify areas for improvement and aspects of the course that resonate well with students.

Time on Task

Measuring students' time on various course-related tasks, especially within online learning platforms, can offer insights into their engagement levels. Extended time spent on tasks could indicate a high level of interest or areas where students may struggle and require additional support.

Metrics for Interaction Quality

Quality of Discussion Contributions

Evaluate the richness, relevance, and depth of student contributions in class discussions and online forums, looking for well-thought-out, relevant responses that stimulate further discussion and demonstrate a deep understanding of the subject matter. To increase student engagement and quality of discussion content, encourage critical thinking and application of concepts through open-ended questions and real-world scenarios. Providing clear guidelines and examples of high-quality contributions can also guide students. Regularly acknowledging and discussing exemplary contributions in class can motivate students to invest more effort and thought into their responses.

Peer-to-Peer Interaction

Assess the extent and quality of student interactions in group activities, collaborative projects, and peer feedback sessions, as effective peer-to-peer interaction often results in more comprehensive learning experiences and reflects a collaborative learning environment. Encourage students to engage constructively and thoughtfully in peer activities, emphasizing the importance of diverse perspectives and respectful dialogue. Best practices for yielding good results include setting clear expectations for interaction, providing structured formats for feedback and discussion, and fostering a supportive atmosphere where students feel comfortable sharing and receiving constructive criticism. Regularly monitor and facilitate these interactions to ensure they remain productive and aligned with learning objectives. Recognize and celebrate effective collaboration and high-quality contributions to reinforce positive behaviors and outcomes.

Instructor-Student Interaction

Monitor the frequency and depth of interactions between instructors and students, focusing on responsiveness to queries and the substantive nature of these exchanges. High-quality instructor-student interactions indicate an active teaching presence and a supportive learning environment. Encourage instructors to engage regularly with students, providing timely and meaningful responses to questions and initiating discussions that deepen understanding. Instructors should also create opportunities for personalized interactions, such as one-on-one consultations or feedback sessions. They can use various communication channels, like emails, forums, or virtual office hours, to ensure student accessibility. Regularly gathering student feedback on the effectiveness of these interactions can guide instructors in enhancing their engagement strategies, fostering a more dynamic and interactive educational experience.

Use of Collaborative Tools

Track the adoption and effectiveness of collaborative tools like shared documents, virtual whiteboards, and discussion forums in facilitating student interactions. Successful integration of these tools typically enhances student engagement and fosters a more interactive learning experience. For instance, sharing documents for group assignments encourages real-time collaboration and idea exchange, while virtual whiteboards can effectively brainstorm sessions during live classes. Discussion forums are ideal for extended, thoughtful discussions, allowing students to engage deeply with the course material and their peers' perspectives. Regularly review and solicit feedback on these tools to understand their impact and explore ways to optimize their use. Encouraging students to use these tools for assignments and informal learning discussions can further enhance their collaborative skills and engagement with the course.

Integrating Analytics Tools

Learning Management System (LMS) Analytics

Analytics tools typically integrated within LMS, or online course platforms can aid educators in gathering comprehensive data on student engagement, participation, and interaction patterns. These tools can provide valuable insights into course dynamics, enabling educators to tailor their teaching methods and course content effectively. Educators can better understand student engagement levels and interaction quality by analyzing data on login frequency, page views, and time spent on specific tasks.

Third-Party Analytics Tools

Education systems may also integrate third-party analytics tools for advanced data collection and analysis. The market offers many such tools and integrates seamlessly into existing platforms. These examples provide insights into the types of tools available and their capabilities, providing insight into what is available.

Analytics Tools

When considering third-party analytics tools for educational purposes, choosing tools that offer robust data collection, user-friendly interfaces, and insightful analysis capabilities is essential. Here are some widely recognized and effective third-party analytics tools that educators, institutions, and online course platforms might consider:

Google Analytics

Best for: Website and LMS traffic analysis.

Features: Tracks and reports website traffic, user engagement, and behavior on educational platforms.

Tableau

Best for: Visualizing complex data.

Features: Offers powerful data visualization tools to make complex analytics more understandable and actionable.

SAS Analytics

Best for: Advanced data analysis.

Features: Provides a range of statistical analysis capabilities, ideal for higher education research and large datasets.

Looker (Part of Google Cloud)

Best for: Integrating data from different sources.

Features: Streamlines data from various sources into understandable reports and dashboards.

Hotjar

Best for: Understanding user experience.

Features: Offers heatmaps, session recordings, and surveys to understand how students interact with online educational content.

Learning Analytics Tools (such as Canvas Analytics or Blackboard Analytics)

Best for: Integration with specific LMS.

Features: These tools are designed to work seamlessly with specific Learning Management Systems, offering insights into student performance and course effectiveness within the LMS.

ZoomInfo

Best for: B2B data for market and audience insights.

Features: It offers comprehensive B2B data that can be valuable for higher education institutions in understanding market trends and audience segmentation.

Qualtrics

Best for: Survey data and student feedback analysis.

Features: An advanced survey tool with powerful analytics to gauge student satisfaction and feedback.

IBM Watson Analytics

Best for: Predictive analysis and AI-powered insights.

Features: Utilizes AI to provide predictive analytics, offering insights into potential future trends and student performance.

When selecting an analytics tool, consider factors such as the specific needs of the educational institution, the type of data being analyzed, user-friendliness, integration capabilities with existing systems, and budget. Each tool has its strengths and is suited to different aspects of educational analytics, from student performance tracking to website and app engagement.

Learning Management Systems Tools

Learning Management Systems (LMS) typically include various built-in tools and features for measuring and evaluating courses, content, and student performance. These tools are essential for educators to monitor the effectiveness of their teaching and for institutions to ensure educational quality. Here are some of the typical performance measurement tools incorporated into LMS systems:

Gradebooks

LMS gradebooks are essential for tracking and recording student grades across various assessments like assignments, quizzes, and exams. These systems allow educators to assign weights to multiple assessments and automatically calculate final grades. This feature provides a clear, continuous record of student performance, helping educators identify trends and areas where students may need additional support or challenge.

Analytics Dashboards

Analytics dashboards in LMS offer comprehensive overviews of student engagement, course completion rates, and individual progress. They visualize data through charts and graphs, making it easier for educators to comprehend and analyze.

These dashboards can highlight general class trends and pinpoint areas where improvements can enhance student outcomes in the course.

Student Participation and Engagement Metrics

LMS systems track metrics like logins, page views, time spent on the platform, and participation in discussions or activities. These metrics are invaluable for identifying students actively engaging with the course material and those at risk of falling behind. They provide educators with the necessary data to intervene effectively and support students' learning journey.

Quiz and Assessment Tools

Quizzes and automated assessment tools in LMS offer immediate feedback, crucial for students learning and understanding. These tools enable educators to gain insights into areas where students excel or struggle, facilitating targeted teaching approaches. They also provide a way to assess and reinforce learning regularly, contributing to a more dynamic and responsive educational experience.

Assignment Submission and Tracking

Manage and track student submissions for assignments: LMS platforms offer robust tools to manage and monitor student assignment submissions. These features often include time-stamping to ensure deadlines are met, originality checking to maintain academic integrity, and integrating grading tools for efficient assessment. The system's ability to organize and archive submissions also aids in keeping a comprehensive record of student work throughout the course.

Course Progress Indicators

Students' progress through course modules: Course progress indicators in LMS systems provide real-time updates on each student's journey through the course. They show the completion of specific sections, modules, or requirements, helping educators gauge how students progress through the material. These indicators are essential for identifying students needing extra support or acceleration.

Feedback Tools

Collect student feedback on courses and instructors: Integrated survey tools in LMS platforms are vital for collecting student feedback. This feedback is invaluable in evaluating the effectiveness of course content and teaching methods. Insights gathered can guide educators in refining their approaches and addressing specific student needs or preferences.

Custom Reports

Generate customizable reports to analyze specific aspects: LMS systems allow educators to create custom reports, focusing on particular areas of student performance or course effectiveness. This feature enables a detailed analysis of various aspects like student engagement, assessment performance, and more, helping educators to focus on areas that require attention or improvement.

Discussion Forum Analysis

Monitor and evaluate student participation in online discussion forums: LMS tools can analyze participation in discussion forums, providing insights into student understanding and engagement with the course material. This analysis helps assess discussions' effectiveness as a learning tool and can guide modifications for increased engagement and insights.

Learning Outcome Tracking

Align course activities and assessments with specific learning outcomes: LMS platforms enable educators to track and report on the achievement of specific learning outcomes. By aligning course activities and assessments with these outcomes, educators can ensure that their teaching effectively meets the educational goals and objectives.

SCORM Compliance and Tracking

SCORM (Sharable Content Object Reference Model) is a set of technical standards developed for e-learning software products. It defines how online learning content and Learning Management Systems (LMS) communicate, allowing LMSs to track learners' progress and performance consistently.

SCORM compliance ensures easy sharing of e-learning content and courses across different systems that adhere to the same model.

How SCORM is Used:
SCORM compliance enables the tracking and reporting of a wide range of data from interactive content and e-learning courses. For example, you can upload a business writing course designed in a SCORM-compliant format to any SCORM-compliant LMS. The system can then track student progress, quiz scores, and completion rates, ensuring a consistent learning experience regardless of the platform used.

Benefits to Learners and Facilitators: SCORM compliance means a seamless and consistent learning experience across various platforms. It simplifies content distribution for course facilitators and offers comprehensive tracking of learner engagement and performance. This data is invaluable in assessing the effectiveness of the course and identifying areas for improvement.

XAPI (Experience API)

XAPI, or Experience API or Tin Can API, is a learning technology specification beyond SCORM's capabilities. It enables tracking various learning experiences outside a traditional LMS, like mobile learning, simulations, and offline activities.

How xAPI Differs from SCORM Unlike SCORM, xAPI can track nearly any learning experience, providing greater flexibility and a more comprehensive understanding of the learner's journey. It collects data about a person's experiences, both online and offline, in a consistent format and stores it in a Learning Record Store (LRS). A Learning Record Store is a specialized data storage system designed to store, share, and retrieve learning records. It is often used with eLearning standards like xAPI (Experience API), which enables online and offline tracking of learning experiences. Different systems can then access this data, allowing for a broader and more integrated view of learning progress.

Benefits and Differences in Tracking xAPI's significant advantage lies in its ability to track many learning experiences and not just e-learning course interactions. It can capture data from simulations, games, social learning, and real-world performance.

For example, in a business writing course, xAPI can track students' completion of e-learning modules and their participation in collaborative writing projects or peer-review exercises, even outside the LMS. This tracking provides a more holistic view of the learning process. It is beneficial for learners seeking a comprehensive record of their experiences and for facilitators aiming to understand the full scope of a student's engagement and learning.

Conclusion: Metrics for Continuous Improvement

By effectively utilizing these key performance metrics, educators and educational leaders can gain valuable insights into the effectiveness of their course content, the level of student engagement, and the quality of interactions. These metrics help assess current courses and guide continuous improvement in future course offerings.

Chapter 19: Discussion Board and Communities

S uccessfully using discussion boards and student communities as engagement activities in an educational setting involves thoughtful planning, active facilitation, and a focus on creating an inclusive and stimulating environment. Here are some strategies to make these tools effective:

Using Discussion Boards Effectively

Using discussion boards and student communities effectively in education requires precise planning, active facilitation, and a focus on inclusivity and engagement. Here is how to maximize the effectiveness of these tools:

Using Discussion Boards Effectively: Clear Guidelines and Objectives

Establish clear, concise guidelines for participation to set expectations on the quality and frequency of posts. Outline specific objectives for discussion board activities, ensuring they are aligned with the course's learning outcomes, to give students a clear understanding of the purpose and value of their contributions.

Structured Discussion Prompts

Design structured, thought-provoking prompts that stimulate critical thinking. Avoid simple yes-or-no questions; open-ended queries encourage diverse viewpoints and in-depth discussion.

This approach helps in fostering a more engaging and intellectually stimulating discussion environment.

Regular Facilitation and Participation

Actively participate in the discussions to steer conversations, inject expert insights, and keep discussions on course. Use follow-up questions to delve deeper into topics, clarify misunderstandings, and connect student comments to the broader course content. This active role helps maintain a focused and meaningful dialogue.

Encourage Peer Interaction

Foster a culture that encourages students to interact with their peers' posts, enhancing peer-to-peer learning and building a community feeling within the course. Acknowledge and commend insightful contributions to motivate deeper engagement among students.

Diverse Discussion Formats

Incorporate a variety of discussion formats, such as debates, case studies, role-playing activities, or reflective posts. This diversity keeps the discussion board dynamic and caters to different learning styles and interests, maintaining high engagement levels.

Timely Feedback

Provide prompt and constructive feedback on student posts. This feedback is crucial for encouraging continuous improvement and showing students their efforts are recognized and valued. It also helps reinforce the learning objectives and align the discussions with course goals.

Building Engaging Student Communities

Creating engaging student communities within an educational setting involves purposeful strategies to foster interaction, collaboration, and a sense of belonging among students.

Purpose-Driven Communities

Develop communities centered around specific course interests, projects, or study topics, providing students with a shared purpose and sense of belonging. This focused approach helps build a solid and engaged community where students are motivated by common goals and interests.

Collaborative Projects

Utilize these communities to facilitate collaborative projects, encouraging students to collaborate, share resources, and provide mutual support. This collaborative environment enhances learning outcomes and fosters teamwork and communication skills essential in real-world settings.

Regular Check-ins and Updates

Organize regular check-ins or updates within the community, where students can discuss their progress, address challenges, or share valuable insights. These sessions help maintain momentum, ensure accountability, and strengthen the sense of community.

Peer Mentoring and Support Groups

Implement peer mentoring within these communities, pairing experienced students with those who are newer or need additional support. This mentorship structure cultivates a nurturing and inclusive learning environment, facilitating knowledge sharing and peer-to-peer support.

Incorporate Multimedia and Interactive Content

Enrich the community experience by incorporating multimedia and interactive content like videos, podcasts, infographics, and interactive discussions. This diversity in content delivery caters to different learning preferences and keeps the community vibrant and engaging.

Recognize and Reward Participation

Acknowledge and celebrate active participation and high-quality contributions within the community. Recognizing individual efforts can significantly boost motivation and encourage ongoing engagement and contribution from all members.

Conclusion: Opportunities for Engagement in Learning

Both discussion boards and student communities can significantly enhance student engagement when used effectively. They provide platforms for deeper exploration of course content, foster a sense of community, encourage peer-to-peer learning, and help students develop critical thinking and communication skills. The key is active facilitation, clear objectives, and a focus on creating an inclusive and intellectually stimulating space.

Chapter 20:
Workshop Engagement

E ngaging students through in-person and online environments requires creative, interactive, and relevant activities. These activities should cater to different learning styles and actively involve students in the learning process. Below are examples aligned with the business course example.

In-Person Engagement Activities

Think-Pair-Share in Business Writing

Example: Students individually brainstorm ideas for a compelling business proposal, discuss them with a partner, and then share their best concepts with the class. This method promotes critical thinking and effective communication strategies in a business context.

Role-Playing in Business Writing

Example: Students role-play as public relations professionals and business clients to practice crafting and delivering press releases. This activity helps them understand the nuances of professional tone and style in business communication.

Interactive Quizzes with Business Writing Content

Use instant quiz sessions with clickers or mobile apps focused on business writing topics. For example, a quiz could test students on different business letter formats or effective email communication strategies, adding an element of fun competition.

Station Teaching for Business Writing Skills

Set up stations focusing on different business writing aspects, such as persuasive writing, report writing, and effective email communication. Students rotate through these stations, engaging in writing exercises and interactive discussions at each point.

Online Engagement Activities

Virtual Think-Pair-Share in Business Writing

Organize virtual breakout rooms where students reflect individually on a business communication case study, discuss in pairs, and share insights with a larger group.

Online Role-Playing for Business Scenarios

Conduct online role-playing sessions where students simulate business negotiations or client meetings via video conferencing. This approach helps in developing practical business communication skills in a virtual setting.

Digital Quizzes and Polls on Business Topics

Implement online quizzes and polls on Kahoot, Google Forms, or other platforms to test students' knowledge of business writing principles. These tools can offer a lively way to review course material and encourage participation, making the learning process more interactive and engaging.

Web-Based Collaborative Projects

Use tools like Google Docs or collaborative project management software to facilitate web-based group projects, where students collaborate to create a comprehensive business plan or marketing strategy. This method enhances teamwork and fosters the practical application of business writing skills in an online environment.

These diverse activities, tailored for in-person and online settings, ensure that students remain engaged and immersed in the learning process, enhancing their understanding and application of the course material.

Class Debates

Organize debates on relevant topics to help students develop their critical thinking, research, and public speaking skills.

An example might be to host debates on topics like "The Role of Email in Modern Business Communication." Students can argue for or against its effectiveness, allowing them to delve into current trends in business writing and develop persuasive communication skills.

Group Projects and Presentations

Students work in groups on a project related to the course content and present their findings. Collaboration may increase the practical application of knowledge.

An example could be to assign students to create a business proposal for a new product or service. They work collaboratively to draft and present the proposal to the class, simulating a real-world business scenario that hones their writing, teamwork, and presentation skills.

Field Trips and Experiential Learning

Field trips to places relevant to the course could be a way to engage students in experiential learning activities that connect academic concepts to real-world experiences.

For example, for the business course, the possibility exists to arrange visits to local businesses where students can observe and analyze real-world business communication strategies. Alternatively, business communication experts can host workshops, designing practical insights and hands-on exercises for effective business writing.

These activities, combining debates, group projects, and experiential learning opportunities, should be designed to provide a comprehensive, engaging, and practical learning experience for students in business writing courses. They enhance the understanding of the course content and prepare students for real-world business communication challenges.

Online Engagement Activities

Virtual Breakout Rooms

Use breakout rooms in video conferencing tools for focused group tasks like drafting different business plan sections. This small group setting encourages active collaboration and idea exchange.

An example related to the business writing course could be to divide students into groups to work on different components of a business proposal, such as market analysis, financial planning, or marketing strategies.

Additional examples:

Role-Playing Negotiations: Assign students in breakout rooms different roles in a corporate scenario, such as buyers and sellers, to practice negotiation skills. They could draft and discuss contracts, proposals, or sale pitches, simulating real-world business negotiations.

Peer Review Sessions: Use breakout rooms for peer-review exercises, where students share and critique each other's business writing drafts, such as emails or reports. This setup allows for more personalized feedback and collaborative editing, enhancing writing skills through constructive peer-to-peer interactions.

Online Discussion Boards

Platforms like Canvas or Moodle can host ongoing discussions on business writing topics, where students can critically engage with the material and each other's viewpoints.

An example of an activity for the business writing course: Post a topic like "The Evolution of Business Communication in the Digital Era" and encourage students to discuss how digital advancements have influenced business writing styles.

Interactive Webinars with Polls and Q&A Sessions

Conduct live webinars on topics like effective business correspondence, using polls for instant feedback, and Q&A sessions for student inquiries.

An example activity could be asking students to host a webinar on crafting persuasive business proposals incorporating polls to understand student preferences on different writing techniques.

Digital Storytelling

Assign projects where students use tools like Adobe Spark or Canva to create digital stories or presentations that explore business writing concepts.

An example assignment could be for students to create a short digital presentation on the fundamental principles of effective business communication, incorporating real-world examples.

Online Simulation Games

Integrate simulation games that enable students to practice and enhance their writing skills in a virtual business environment. Such games demonstrate how effective business writing can boost a business's visibility. For example, create a simulation game where students act as public relations specialists for a virtual corporation. In this game, they draft press releases, handle customer inquiries via email, and develop communication strategies for various scenarios, such as product launches or handling public relations crises. This simulation offers practical experience crafting effective business communication tailored to different audiences and situations.

Other examples include:

Crisis Management Simulation: Implement a game where students manage a crisis in a virtual company, requiring them to draft urgent communications to various stakeholders, including press releases and internal memos.

Project Management Exercise: Introduce a simulation where students act as project managers, coordinating with virtual team members and stakeholders. They could write project proposals and progress reports and demonstrate how to manage client communications effectively.

Peer Review and Feedback Sessions

Organize online sessions where students share their business writing drafts and receive constructive feedback from peers.

Example: Students submit their business email drafts for peer review, focusing on clarity, tone, and effectiveness. Peer review assignments can be very successful with students working together through respectful comments to benefit each other's assignments.

Virtual Scavenger Hunts

Create an online scavenger hunt where students find and analyze real-world examples. The discipline of engaging in real-world examples provides an opportunity for students to test and refine their searching skills while also finding relevant content.

An example for the business writing course could be where students can use published content to search for and critique examples of effective and poor business communication found in online articles, reports, or corporate websites.

These online engagement activities, tailored for a business writing course, offer diverse and interactive ways to deepen students' understanding of course content. By varying these activities, educators can ensure a dynamic and engaging online learning environment catering to different learning styles and preferences.

Conclusion: Engagement

Both in-person and online educational environments provide distinct opportunities for engaging students effectively. The key to successful student engagement lies in selecting activities that align with the course or workshop's overarching learning objectives and cater to students' diverse needs and learning styles. By incorporating various activities— from interactive discussions and collaborative projects to digital storytelling and simulation games—we can ensure that the learning experience remains dynamic and interactive. This varied approach is crucial in maintaining high student engagement and participation levels, ultimately leading to a more enriching and effective educational journey. Whether in a traditional classroom setting or virtual learning space, the adaptability and diversity of engagement strategies are instrumental in creating an impactful and memorable learning experience for all students. Generative AI can help design these experiences, creating creative opportunities aligning with the course objectives.

Chapter 21:
Embracing the AI Revolution

A As we close this insightful journey on the evolution of education, we reflect on generative AI's profound implications and opportunities in the educational landscape. This book intended to provide an understanding of generative AI and practical strategies and tools for integrating it into educational content and workshop development. Learning Management Systems will continue to evolve with more integration of AI influencing their development.

Key Takeaways

Generative AI as a Transformative Tool

Generative AI represents a fundamental shift in the educational landscape, transcending traditional content creation, delivery, and student interaction methods. Its implementation marks a significant leap forward, offering innovative approaches to teaching and learning. By embracing this technology, educators can revolutionize how educational content is developed and experienced, making it more dynamic, effective, and tailored to the evolving needs of students and the educational sector.

Personalization and Engagement

The ability of AI to provide highly personalized learning experiences is one of its most groundbreaking features. AI's capacity to tailor content to each student's needs, learning styles, and progress is transformative. The level of personalization, combined with engaging, interactive activities, significantly enhances student involvement and motivation. Embracing these capabilities in course and workshop development can lead to more effective learning outcomes and a more engaging educational journey.

Ethical Considerations and Legal Compliance

Incorporating AI into education requires careful navigation of ethical and legal territories. Ethical considerations, such as data privacy, bias prevention, and the impact on traditional teaching roles, are paramount. Likewise, adherence to legal standards, including compliance with regulations like GDPR and FERPA, is crucial. Understanding and addressing these aspects are essential to ensuring AI's responsible and beneficial use in educational settings. As educators harness the potential of AI, prioritizing these considerations will be instrumental in building trust and integrity in AI-enhanced education.

Continuous Learning and Adaptation

Educators and developers must embrace continuous learning to keep up with the rapid advancements in AI. Understanding the evolving nature of AI technologies and their applications in education is vital for maintaining effective and relevant teaching methods. As AI evolves, so should the approaches used in educational settings, ensuring they meet the changing needs of learners and the education sector.

Next Steps: Embrace a Culture of Experimentation

Start small with AI and explore a variety of tools. Experimentation is crucial for understanding AI's potential and limitations in an educational context. This method enables gradual scaling and refinement of using AI, enhancing confidence and expertise.

Focus on Skill Development

Skills like AI literacy and data interpretation are critical for creating and managing AI-driven educational content. A firm grasp of ethical AI use is also essential, ensuring responsible and effective content management.

Leverage Community and Collaboration

Participate in professional communities and collaborative AI projects as they can offer valuable insights and innovative approaches. Engaging with peers in these settings enriches the educational experience and fosters a broader understanding of AI in education.

Monitoring and Evaluating Continuously and Regularly

Assessing the impact of AI on educational content is crucial for continuous improvement. Feedback and performance metrics should guide course and workshop development refinement, using AI tools and strategies and ensuring they align with educational objectives.

Stay Informed and Agile

Keeping content relevant and compelling is essential to stay informed about the latest AI developments and educational methodologies. Adaptability and responsiveness to new trends are necessary for maintaining a cutting-edge educational approach.

Prioritize Ethics and Accessibility

Ensuring that AI-driven educational initiatives are inclusive, equitable, and ethically sound is paramount. Prioritizing these aspects guarantees that all learners can access and benefit from AI in education, fostering a just and fair learning environment.

Looking Ahead: The Future of AI in Education

As we look towards the future, it is clear that generative AI will continue to play a significant role in shaping educational experiences. The journey of integrating AI into education, whether synchronous or asynchronous learning, hybrid, or workshop style, is ongoing and dynamic. The success of this integration will largely depend on our ability to understand and harness these technologies thoughtfully and creatively.

This book is a beacon for those navigating this new terrain. It offers the tools, insights, and inspiration needed to effectively utilize generative AI, transforming how we teach, learn, and think about education in the AI era. The future is here and is ripe with possibilities for those ready to embrace the AI revolution in education.

Closing Thoughts

The rapid evolution of AI technologies presents a landscape rich with opportunities and challenges, necessitating a commitment to ongoing learning and adaptation. As the author, my dedication to advancing this topic remains unwavering with continued work to delve deeper into the nuances of AI in educational settings, engaging in continuous learning, speaking at various forums, and writing to share insights and developments. The commitment to stay at the forefront of AI advancements is not just a professional pursuit but a passion to contribute meaningfully to transforming educational paradigms.

The importance of staying current in this swiftly changing field cannot be overstated. As educators, content creators, and leaders in the learning community, we must actively embrace these technological advancements. Staying informed, adapting to new tools and methodologies, and integrating AI into our educational practices is no longer a choice but a necessity. Do not be left behind by these rapid changes. Technology and education are increasingly intertwined. Let us move forward with an open mind, ready to embrace the transformative power of AI, and continue to shape a future of education that is innovative, inclusive, and profoundly effective.

Chapter 22: Resources

Guide to AI Resources for Educators

T his chapter serves as a resource, offering educators a curated list of websites, online courses, platforms, and tools for further learning and exploration more broadly with the topic of AI. These resources aim to enhance understanding, skill development, and practical application of AI in educational settings.

Websites and Online Platforms

OpenAI (https://www.openai.com)

A leading AI research and deployment company providing the latest research, publications, and tools like ChatGPT and DALL-E.

Open Learning (https://openlearning.ai4all.org)

Provides open-access resources and curriculum focused on teaching AI to high school students.

Kaggle (https://www.kaggle.com)

A platform for data science competitions and a resource for datasets, notebooks, and AI and machine learning tutorials.

Coursera (https://www.coursera.org)

Offers a range of online courses and specializations in AI and machine learning from top universities and companies.

edX (https://www.edx.org)

Provides online courses in AI and related fields from leading institutions like MIT and Harvard.

Google AI (https://ai.google)

Google offers resources, tools, and research on AI and machine learning.

MIT OpenCourseWare (https://ocw.mit.edu)

Free course materials from MIT, including AI, machine learning, and computer science courses.

Online Courses

AI for Everyone (Coursera)

A beginner-level course that provides a broad introduction to AI.

Deep Learning Specialization (Coursera)

A series of courses that delve deeper into the concepts of deep learning and neural networks.

Introduction to TensorFlow (Coursera)

Focuses on using TensorFlow, a tool for machine learning and AI applications.

Machine Learning (edX)

A course offered by Columbia University that covers machine learning concepts and algorithms.

Tools and Software for Generative AI

TensorFlow (https://www.tensorflow.org)

An open-source platform for machine learning and AI development.

PyTorch (https://pytorch.org)

An open-source machine learning library for Python used for applications in AI.

Hugging Face (https://huggingface.co)

Provides a range of pre-trained models and tools for natural language processing tasks.

Scratch (https://scratch.mit.edu)

A visual programming language and online community aimed at younger students for creating interactive stories, games, and animations.

Professional Networks and Communities

AI in Education Society (https://aiedsociety.org)

A professional society focused on advancing AI in education through research and practice.

Association for the Advancement of Artificial Intelligence (https://www.aaai.org)

An international organization promoting research in and responsible use of artificial intelligence.

LinkedIn Groups: AI in Education

Professional groups on LinkedIn where educators can connect, share, and learn about AI in education.

Note: Sites and links change from time to time, and as of this writing, this information is current but subject to change or removal.

Conclusion: A Gateway to AI Learning

This directory provides a starting point for educators to dive into the world of AI, offering a range of resources for various levels of expertise and interest. Staying updated with these resources can help educators integrate AI into their teaching practices and remain at the forefront of this rapidly evolving field.

Chapter 23:
Vendor Directory for Course Development

Partnering with Vendors for Enhanced Online Learning

T he industry is evolving to meet educators' and educational leaders' needs. Below is a select, curated list of vendors specializing in online course development. There are many more vendors, and an Internet search can produce more results. These vendors include those involved with course content creation, audio and video production, and integration solutions for complete course delivery.

Vendors for Online Course Content Creation

Coursera Content Partners

Description: Partners with universities and organizations to create high-quality online courses.

Services: Comprehensive course design, including curriculum development and instructional design.

Coursera for Business

https://www.coursera.org/business

Udemy for Business

https://business.udemy.com

Description: Offers a platform for experts to create and sell courses, focusing on professional and personal development.

Services: Course creation tools, market insights, and support for instructors. Search for each website noted below to understand more about their offerings.

Khan Academy Creator

https://www.khanacademy.org/

Description: Known for educational courses, particularly in STEM fields.

Services: Course content development with an emphasis on interactive learning.

Vendors for Audio and Video Content Production

TechSmith

https://www.techsmith.com/

Description: Specializes in software for creating video tutorials and educational content.

Services: Tools for screen recording, video editing, and interactive content creation.

Products: Camtasia, Snagit

Adobe Creative Cloud

https://www.adobe.com/creativecloud.html

Description: Offers a suite of tools for graphic design, video editing, and web development.

Services: Industry-standard tools for high-quality audio and video production.

Products: Adobe Premiere Pro, After Effects, Audition

Animoto

https://animoto.com/

Description: Provides easy-to-use tools for creating professional videos.

Services: Video creation platform with customizable templates and a library of stock photos and music.

Articulate Storyline

https://www.articulate.com/

Description: Provides a software tool used for creating interactive e-learning courses.

Services: Storyline enables the creation of custom, interactive content that can include quizzes, simulations, and branching scenarios. It supports a range of multimedia elements, such as audio, video, and animation.

Lectora

https://www.elblearning.com/create-learning/lectora

Description: a software tool used for creating interactive e-learning courses.

Services: Storyline enables the creation of custom, interactive content that can include quizzes, simulations, and branching scenarios. It supports a range of multimedia elements, such as audio, video, and animation.

Vendors for Course Integration Solutions

Canvas by Instructure

https://www.instructure.com/canvas

Description: A popular learning management system (LMS) for educational institutions.

Services: Course hosting, student tracking, grade management, and integration with various educational tools.

Blackboard Learn

https://www.blackboard.com/

Description: Offers a comprehensive suite of online course management and delivery tools.

Services: LMS with features for course content delivery, assessments, and student engagement.

Moodle

https://moodle.org/

Description: An open-source learning platform designed to provide educators with tools to create personalized learning environments.

Services: Extensive customization options and a vast community for support and plugins.

Conclusion: Streamlining Online Course Development

By partnering with these vendors, educators and educational institutions can access specialized tools and services to create, enhance, and deliver high-quality online courses. Each vendor offers unique capabilities, enabling educators to choose solutions that best fit their course objectives and student needs.

Additional Resources

Adobe. (2023). "Adobe Creative Cloud for Education". Retrieved from Adobe Creative Cloud

AI Education Association. (2023). "Best Practices in AI-Enabled Education". AIEA Publications.

Amanda R. Ellis & Emily Slade (2023) A New Era of Learning: Considerations for ChatGPT as a Tool to Enhance Statistics and Data Science Education, Journal of Statistics and Data Science Education, 31:2, 128-133, DOI: 10.1080/26939169.2023.2223609

Canvas LMS. (2023). Canvas LMS: AI Integration. Retrieved from Canvas LMS Website

Chen, Su-Yen. "Generative AI, Learning and New Literacies." Journal of Educational Technology Development and Exchange 16, no. 2 (2023): 1–19.

Coursera Business. (2023). "Creating Courses with Industry Experts". Retrieved from Coursera for Business

Denny, Paul, Juho Leinonen, James Prather, Andrew Luxton-Reilly, Thezyrie Amarouche, Brett A Becker, and Brent N Reeves. "Prompt Problems: A New Programming Exercise for the Generative AI Era." arXiv.org (2023).

Dickey, Ethan, and Andres Bejarano. "A Model for Integrating Generative AI into Course Content Development." arXiv.org (2023).

Elsayed, Saber. "Towards Mitigating ChatGPT's Negative Impact on Education: Optimizing Question Design Through Bloom's

Taxonomy." In 2023 IEEE Region 10 Symposium (TENSYMP), 1–6. IEEE, 2023.

European Commission. (2023). General Data Protection Regulation (GDPR). Retrieved from GDPR Website

Federal Trade Commission. (2023). Children's Online Privacy Protection Act (COPPA). Retrieved from COPPA Website

Goddard, M. (2017). The EU General Data Protection Regulation (GDPR): European Regulation that has a Global Impact. International Journal of Market Research, 59(6), 703-705. https://doi-org.du.idm.oclc.org/10.2501/IJMR-2017-050

Google AI. (2023). Google Colab Tutorials. Retrieved from Google Colab Resources

Ilieva, Galina, Tania Yankova, Stanislava Klisarova-Belcheva, Angel Dimitrov, Marin Bratkov, and Delian Angelov. "Effects of Generative Chatbots in Higher Education." Information (Basel) 14, no. 9 (2023): 492-.

Instructure. (2023). "Canvas LMS: The Learning Management System of Choice for Schools"

Johnson, L. (2023). "Adaptive Learning Technologies in Higher Education". University Press.

King, Stephen, and Judhi Prasetyo. "\Assessing generative AI through the lens of the Gartner Technology Hype Cycle: a collaborative autoethnography." In Frontiers in Education, vol. 8, p. 1300391. Frontiers.

LinkedIn Groups. (2023). AI in Education Group. Retrieved from LinkedIn

Nilsson, N.J. (1995), Eye on the Prize. AI Magazine, 16: 9-17. https://doi-org.du.idm.oclc.org/10.1609/aimag.v16i2.1129

OpenAI. (2023). ChatGPT: Optimizing Language Models for Dialogue. Retrieved from OpenAI Website

OpenAI. (2023). DALL-E: Creating Images from Text. Retrieved from OpenAI Website References

Popovici, Matei-Dan. "ChatGPT in the Classroom. Exploring Its Potential and Limitations in a Functional Programming Course." International Journal of Human-Computer Interaction (2023): 1–12.

Ramirez, Clifford A. FERPA Clear and Simple: The College Professional's Guide to Compliance. 1. Aufl. Newark: Jossey-Bass, 2009.

Sarkar, Hiranmay, and Sourav Saha. "Generative AI: Gold Rush or Bust?" Supply Chain Management Review 27, no. 5 (2023): 10–13.

Smith, J., & Doe, A. (2023). "Innovative Course Design with AI". Journal of Educational Technology.

U.S. Department of Education. (2023). Family Educational Rights and Privacy Act (FERPA). Retrieved from FERPA Website

Yilmaz, Ramazan, and Fatma Gizem Karaoglan Yilmaz. "The Effect of Generative Artificial Intelligence (AI)-Based Tool Use on Students' Computational Thinking Skills, Programming Self-Efficacy and Motivation." Computers and education. Artificial intelligence 4 (2023): 100147-.

Willey, Lorrie, Barbara Jo White, and Cynthia S. Deale. "Teaching AI in the College Course: Introducing the AI Prompt Development Life Cycle (PDLC)." Issues in Information Systems 24, no. 2 (2023).

About the Author

Dr. Debora Bartoo, a seasoned payments executive in financial services, actively applies her extensive knowledge to the payments industry and the academic realm. She holds a Ph.D. from Antioch University and incorporates innovative techniques into teaching, seamlessly blending her expertise with educational advancements. In addition to her Ph.D., her academic credentials include a Master of Science in Leadership in Organizations focusing on innovation from the University of Pennsylvania and a Master of Science in Business Analytics from St. Joseph's University. These qualifications enable her to effectively integrate innovative knowledge and skills into teaching today's workforce.

Dr. Bartoo stands out as an industry expert in the field of payments, where her many years in financial services provided the opportunity to lead payments workshops. She also teaches master's level university courses in innovation, strategy, values-driven decision-making, environmental scanning, and the capstone research-based course. She also designs online coursework to aid with upskilling employees. Her commitment to education extends beyond the classroom, as she actively contributes to the community through various university appointments and management committees. Her industry experience and academic insights make her an asset in the corporate and academic worlds, offering real-world relevance and transformative educational experiences.

www.ingramcontent.com/pod-product-compliance
Lightning Source LLC
Chambersburg PA
CBHW060526130626
46553CB00002B/666